"- - - and GULLIVER RETURNS."

--In Search of Utopia--

Book One

REVERSING OVERPOPULATION
The Planet's Doomsday Threat

Lemuel Gulliver XVI

". . . AND GULLIVER RETURNS"
--In Search of Utopia--

BOOK 1 REVERSING OVERPOPULATION

--The Planet's Doomsday Threat—

by
Lemuel Gulliver XVI as told to Jacqueline Slow

© 2016 Total Health Publications

By the way, as most of you know, we have put our photos before every bit of dialogue.

This should make you more familiar with us. So these books read more like plays. Since most of you read the books in PDF or EPUB format it is no problem. But if you read them in RTF or TXT you will probably lose the photos. This will make the transitions of the conversations more difficult to follow.

When read as ebooks, which are free to the concerned readers of the world, the table of contents will have no page number because different book sales organizations use different technologies so that the pages will not be consistent from one seller to another. In ebooks just search the terms you want in the search field. If you read it as a pdf file or a print book the table of contents will have page numbers.

You will notice when reading that the odd numbered books, while heavily documented, may seem like a combination of science fiction and non-fiction. They chronicle our travels. However the even numbered books are non-fiction and explore one or more issues introduced in the previous book..

As we explore the issues that threaten our planet, I hope you become as concerned as I am.   If you have any comment on my thoughts please contact me at: mailto:gulliverreturns@gmail.com   LG

TABLE OF CONTENTS

THE RETURN FROM SPACE

4-3-2-1-Touch down! . . . and Gulliver returns. The greatest adventure in human history! Commander Lemuel Gulliver the 16th has completed the first journey around the solar system. Today, May 17, 2025 is a day that will be forever engraved in the minds of humanity.

    "This is Chet Rowland of World News on the California desert where we have just witnessed the final leg of the greatest human adventure in history, even greater than that of his illustrious ancestor, Lemuel Gulliver the First. After 25 years in space, Lemuel Gulliver the 16th returns from his odyssey of exploring most of the solar system in search of possible homes for the billions of earthlings who have overflowed our planet. Let me try to grab him on his way to de-briefing.

    "Commander, let me just ask a couple of questions that the waiting world wants to know."

Sure, but I only have a minute"

"Have you found suitable potential homes for the excess world population?

    "Not at all. There are a few places on Mars and Venus that might be suitable for underground cities. But there is no place in our solar system as 'people friendly' as our own Earth."

    "What made you volunteer for the trip and were you ever sorry that you did? And were you lonely?"

    "it was two pronged. First, there was the problem that we had gotten ourselves into in terms of overpopulation-- which is responsible for climate change, youth unemployment and violence, both terrorism and street violence. It has been clearly shown that if there are too many people who have not had a strong family upbringing and adequate education they are more likely to become antisocial. It happens in the poor areas of our cities and countries and results terrorism—from the youth and adult gangs in most countries to be more organized anti-western terrorists like ISIS and its lookalike counterparts throughout the world.

    "It is not only the overpopulation, but the under-preparedness of so many parents in the world to have children. Most of the problems in the world today are related to too many people and too few who have been parented effectively.

"You would think that as we became more knowledgeable we would anticipate the problems earlier. A few could see that Hitler was evil and was bad for Germany. A few saw that our lax loan procedures would result in the recession of 2008. Malthus and Ehrlich were among the small minority predicting overpopulation and its problems. Why can't we predict the obvious and prevent the calamities that the seers have seen?

"Our citizens and our politicians become aware of problems and try to solve them long after they are unsolvable. Most of us see the present as acceptable and hold out the hope for a better tomorrow. But few work for tomorrow. Most feel no need to turn off their video games and televisions. Politicians should solve our problems—as long as they don't raise our taxes.

"If we solved the problem of renewable energy for the whole world today we could not expect our climate to return to normal for 100 years. We see poorly parented young adults in the world committing terrible atrocities. If we catch them we put them in prison. This costs society much more than if they had prevented them in his youth—by effective loving and by an exceptional education.. We are always too late in planning as individuals and as societies. We spend huge amounts of time, money and resources to try to solve the problems that we could have prevented.

"My second reason for being excited about such a trip was my joy in adventure. Like my famous ancestor, the first Gulliver, I lusted for adventure. But the adventure into the unknown world by his sailing ship 300 years ago could not have been as exciting as the lure of other worlds beyond our world. The thrill of space travel and being the first person to set foot on several planets gave me orgasmic thrills that will live with me every day of my life.

"As I said a major reason for the trip was to solve our overpopulation problem. I became aware of the problems of overpopulation when I read Rachel Carson's "Silent Spring" and Paul Ehrlich's "Population Bomb." I knew that something had to be done. Some people had suggested that we move people to other planets. I was offered the chance to find out if it was feasible. We also wanted to know more about our solar system. It was an outstanding opportunity to look at solving our greatest human problem and at the same time contribute to the knowledge that has puzzled us for millenia. How could I refuse such an opportunity?

"And you ask was I lonely. Yes and no. I enjoy human companionship as the most soothing and stimulating salve to my soul. But I was not alone. I had with me Plato and Aristotle, Jesus and Mohammed, Lao Tzu and Confucius, Galileo and Copernicus, Freud and Bacon, Shakespeare and Milton. I was never alone. My 25 years in space gave me years of uninterrupted reading time to study the great books of our world. And that voyage into our intellectual cosmos was at least as exciting as my travel in space. It gave me both the hope of possible solutions to our planetary problems and a fear that human selfishness would continue to prevent them.

"I had a lot of time to think about other issues that impede our enjoying and contributing to our world. A major question for me became whether happiness of the population should be a major, or THE major, goal of governments.

"I certainly think that every government I have seen is not primarily concerned with the health and happiness of its citizens. Their concern is more for increasing economic output-- or income from grants, as we often see in Africa from the West and from China. Much of that income then goes into the pockets of the ruling class or into the profits of the Western companies that provide the goods and services. Corruption is everywhere! And it steals from the people.

"I wonder why the accumulation of money is more important than happiness. We want low taxes for ourselves, but accept multi-million dollar salaries for CEOs and entertainers like pro athletes, film stars and some singers. Athletes make up to $200 million a year for kicking or hitting a ball-- or each other. A major reason that healthcare costs are so high in the US is that the CEOs of health insurance companies make $5-$10 million a year. Compare that with the $100,000 to $200,000 that the bureaucrats make in the welfare countries for doing the same job. The heads of Oracle make about $53 million a year—but they are not entertainers so they shouldn't be overpaid. Oracle is at least making things that how are modern world needs. Does the world really need somebody who throws touchdown passes, hits pointers, scores an occasional soccer goal, has a good left jab or can pretend that he is somebody else next film?

"When I think of the Roman poet Juvenal's observation of 2000 years ago that the people are content if they are given bread and circuses, I understand why the population and the governments foster this entertainment. It keeps people's minds off of the ineptitude and corruption of so many of their leaders. They certainly do not want educated people because educated people will know a bit about what is necessary for today's and tomorrow's world.

 "You were out in space when President Obama suggested his health care plan. He wanted a federal option for insurance that would have cut expenses way down for the consumer. Insurance company lobbies shot that down buy rewarding congressman with huge amounts of extra money for their campaigns. The president wanted a maximum medical malpractice award of $250,000. The lawyers lobbies shot that down. I like to call our government a lobbyocracy rather than a democracy. With the cost of running for Congress every two years at a million dollars and the cost of running for a Senate seat at about $5,000,000 our representatives did you spend are great deal of time raising money by selling their votes to lobbyists and special interest groups. In no other country is such corruption legal. PamHow important it is to keep our 'do nothing' representative in office so that no challenger, no matter how qualified, has much of a chance to be elected. With gerrymandered congressional districts and our representatives selling their votes—it is no wonder that our country it is so ineffective in delivering happiness and contentment to the taxpayers."

"Amen! I think we should consider happiness, rather than low taxes, and as a goal for society. The few countries that rank highest in happiness are in Scandinavia, Western Europe and Oceania. Taxes are always higher in the happier countries. Higher taxes yield better healthcare for less money, free education to the doctoral level, more secure pensions, more vacation time, fully paid extended parental leave for 10 to 12 months after a birth, and a number of other perks that seems to make people happier. In our country, the good old US of A, we rank 10th in the world's happiness ratings. We pay 2 to 3 times more than any other country for healthcare, but our health care system is ranked 40th in the world. Our college students go into significant debts which often take many years to pay off. The average medical doctor amasses almost a half million dollars in debt before being ready to practice medicine. In America we get 2 to 3 weeks vacation commonly, while our European friends get 4 to 6 weeks. No wonder they are happier than we are. Of course our taxes are lower. We would have to increase our taxes by 50% in order to be happier! But Americans know that after they die they can take their bankbooks with them to that Big Stockmarket in the Sky.

"Our problems are many. Here are a few that I see:

- Overpopulation;
- Poor parenting;
- A generally ineffective educational system run by locally elected people who may have no knowledge of what a quality education is;
- The lack of recognition that today we not only need a very high level of technical education but we also need more general education and more work in the humanities;
- A huge reduction in the jobs necessary to run the world because of computers, robotics and 3D printing;
- People expecting the government to fix all the problems while not taking responsibility for their own lives and the lives of the future inhabitants of our world;
- Relying on democratic votes when the voters are not properly aware of the issues. When the people of the UK voted 52% to 48% to leave the European Union, did they all have the same factual information on the issue?;
- The nearly universal drive for power-- which grows if the ability to love is not nourished, is a cancer to our world through wars, terrorism, abuse, racism and hate—cannot be remedied until all children have capable and loving parents;
- The selfishness, which is natural in infants, will remain in any adults who are not loved by their caretakers and who do not have their basic physical and psychological needs met.needs met.
- The essential requirement for our basic physical and psychological needs to be met results in radical adjustments such as withdrawing from society through the pleasure of psychoactive drugs or by attacking society through such actions as child abuse and terrorism.

"These are but a few of the problems of our modern world. I plan to visit several countries, many of whom have addressed one or more of these problems and have solved them. I wonder if the drive for power or if selfishness is the most basic issue that needs to be addressed.

"Plato saw the selfishness of the family as preventing the best of societies. The Soviet Union's failure to establish a Communist utopia hinged on a combination of human frailties— the economic selfishness of the masses, the power-mad leaders and the universal propensity to prepare for and recover from war. Plato's city-state and Bacon's island state were too small to be useful as models for today's multi-billion population with space age communication, a global economy, and a myriad of religions and philosophies that divide our human brotherhood into billions of Cains and Abels. Still we should heed the advice of the king of New Atlantis and work to join humanity and policy together.

"Today our overpopulation chokes our skies and our seas with our solid and aerosol wastes. We have changed our climate—heating it to temperatures too warm for comfort, drying our fields and sucking water vapor into the air that sometimes results in droughts— sometimes in massive storms that cost us thousands of lives and billions of dollars.

"There are so many problems. Selfishness, ignorance and the lack of the ability to love are fundamental to most of our problems. We see selfishness in the young and old. We expect it in the young but we would hope that we would be able to see with enlightened self interest as we grow older. But we see in our democracies that old people vote for larger pensions, earlier retirement and more medical treatments free. Very often they voted for lower taxes when they were working but now they want more benefits from somebody else's taxes. The good of society would require cheaper and better education for the young. We live much longer than ever but we refuse to be responsible for our retirements. Governments cannot pay for the extra years that we live but did not pay for in our retirement contributions."

"Yes commander, I saw that recently in Norway where the Opera's pension system was unable to pay the dancers, who retired at 41, and the singers, who retired at 52. Their generous welfare system did not require them to bring their expertise into another area if they could no longer dance or sing. Others, like professors, had to retire at 67 or 70, even if they wanted to work. Absurd! I know a couple of teachers in California who worked well into their 90s—and one was a multi-millionaire.

"But I can understand wanting to retire if you are in a boring job."

"My point exactly. Chet. A major concern of mine is the inability of so many parents to love their children effectively. As love was defined in the Encyclopedia of Mental Health by Ashley Montagu, love is the ability to do what is best for the other person. Certainly parents must understand the basics of nutrition so that they can feed their children properly. They certainly need enough money to buy the food and adequately house the child. They need an appreciation of child psychology so that they can understand and help their children at each age. They should have a good educational background, or at least an appreciation of the importance of education for their children.

"These are not simple tasks, in fact I wonder if any parent has all these skills and abilities! I'm quite sure that 16 year old unmarried mothers and drug addicts don't have them. Parents who perform 'honor killings' of their daughters because they don't obey the family traditions are also lacking. How about the parents of the jihadist terrorists? Do you think they effectively loved their children? Do you think a truly loved person would shoot or behead an innocent person?

" Climate change is even related to an increase in violence, according to studies at Princeton and The University of California. (1) But I think that it is the overpopulation that is causing both.

"Our excess billions of mouths thirst for fresh water that cowers deeper and deeper into the womb of Mother Earth. Our advanced medical technology lengthens our lifespans while industrial technology makes us less necessary as workers. We see national unemployment levels of 10 to over 25% and youth unemployment at twice that level. We no longer need a pair of bodies to operate the butcher shop, the cheese shop, the bakery or the fruit shop. One tenth the number can operate the supermarket and give us an even better selection and service. We don't need an assembly line of people bolting fenders on cars. Computerized robots do it now. 3D printing replaces many machine operators and engineers as it significantly reduces the time and effort necessary to develop prototypes. We don't need a subsistence farmer tilling behind his mule or bullock. A machine can do the work of thousands of subsistence farmers."

"Very true. I guess everyone on the planet needs a university education now."

"To be employed it is certainly more necessary today. But there are two major considerations. One is the quality of the education, the other is what is studied. I don't think you'll have a lot of trouble employing people in any field from UCLA, Stanford or the Ivy League schools or from Oxford or Cambridge. People from effective universities in engineering, physics, IT and other needed skills shouldn't have problems—although the 'for profit' schools have a terrible reputation in every field. Students pay their excessive tuition, borrow from the government to pay it, get the good grades they have paid for, but then they don't qualify for the jobs they want. Employers want the best people--and the best people qualified for the better schools--which usually have lower tuition than the 'for profits.'

"So many students want to study in fields of their interest—philosophy, art history, sociology, sport science and so forth. These certainly will make them well-rounded educated citizens, but their employability is severely limited. Our global economy needs salable skills—and the studies that give us a well-rounded education may not make us employable in the technical fields where the jobs are. Psychology is a fascinating field of study, but it has the absolute worst prospects for landing a job.

"This brings me to another concern. Not only are people allowed to retire before they have contributed enough to pay for their retirements. Their increased life expectancy has not been factored into the actuarial tables used for retirements. Additionally many countries require retirement between 65 and 70 and lose talented and experienced people who can help to solve society's problems while they don't require their governments to borrow from China to pay for their retirements. Governments continually enact laws that are counter-productive to protecting our ecology, our economies, our safety and our happiness.

"We should be guided by the practice of the rulers of Bacon's utopia New Atlantis. Voyagers would set out periodically to bring back the knowledge of other civilizations to make their own kingdom better. The arts and sciences, the inventions and manufactures, the books and instruments were shared—making every civilization richer. Because, after all, as Bacon said 'knowledge is power.' Such a worldly endeavor appeals to me now. I think there is the possibility to save ourselves from ourselves.

"And we need better education for all the people. Today people specialize so much that they don't know anything about other fields. Did you know that few economists have any biological or chemical studies in their college degree programs. Most think that economic production is what the world is about. Is making money more important than survival?

"In space I kept up with a Stanford University program that kept me focused on what is important. Check out mahb.stanford.edu. If you are not yet concerned with survival, it will put you on track."

"It is a great site—I read it all the time. I wish the politicians and business leaders would read it and take it to heart.

"What are your immediate plans now that you've rejoined humanity?"

"Some might think that I would want to take a month on Tahiti and soak up some rays, but remember, I have been alone for 25 years. I want to jump into the chaos of civilization and visit some countries that interest me. Some countries have made effective strides in solving our universal problems. I have only been able to hear about the movements, both positive and negative, that nations have taken to grapple with humankind's greatest problem—overpopulation. I want to see for myself. We're choking ourselves with our wastes in the air, in the ground and in the seas. We live in fear of criminals, terrorists and warlords—warlords who have gained power through ballots or bullets. Utopia is a realizable dream, but will we decide to pursue it?"

"I have planned to visit both rich and poor countries to see how they are attempting to dam the flood of overpopulation. I want to understand the ethical and psychological barriers to reversing our planetary curse (Books 4 and 6) and I want to look at the myriad of methods that have been used to motivate or coerce us in so many ways and try to understand which methods might be best used to motivate our world's population to climb out of the pit of tradition that ties us to the past.(Book 8) Our present and future require that we quickly reverse population growth, Further, as we see the number of anti-social people in our midst, I want to see what is being done to increase eu-parenting. It is obvious to all informed people that our population must be reduced and that our advanced weapon technology gives terrorists and psychotics the means to kill and maim hundreds or thousands of innocent people. Others of their ilk destroy women and children thru rape, enslavement or other sexual harassing and abusing behaviors. Too many of our brethren are anti-social. I think that better parenting can reduce this inhumanity.

"But my concerns have gone even farther afield. My reading makes me wonder about the understandings on which most modern states use for governing. Do we want economic success, then we might follow China's socialistic-capitalistic Communist Party oligarchy. If happiness for the citizens is the goal we might follow the highly taxed Denmark. They like to put the idea of 'play' into most area of their lives—including work. I have been lucky in my adult life in enjoying all of my work—as a lifeguard, professor and recently as an astronaut. But in my home country it seems that the major concern is in keeping taxes low. I really don't understand how they want the world's major defense force, adequate pensions and better medical care without paying for it. Our lobby-ocracy's power seems to work in opposition to the good of the people.

"Why is it that Denmark, with a tax rate 40% higher than that of the U.S., is rated as the world's happiest country while the U.S, is eleventh. In fact all the happiest countries had tax rates far above that of the U.S. I read this in the Los Angeles Times in a report of the United Nations based on a number of different polls such as Gallup and Pew.

"So I want to look at as many problems facing our world as I can. It seems that so many are interrelated—like overpopulation and unemployment; uneducated parents and their uneducated children and youth unemployment; increasing lifespans and underfunded retirement plans;

More social welfare or defense spending without taxing for it; the problem of determining what is 'just' when we attempt to develop modern societies on the often conflicting ideals of liberty and equality (Books 9, 10, 11); and the positive and negative influences of religions on the world's societies.

"I don't think you can do it all in one lifetime! But we could hope that with that whole solar system out there, there might be some possibility of finding a place for utopian settlements to be developed?"

"No, not with our present technology—the possibility just isn't there. We have found specks of water on our moon and on Enceladus, one of Saturn's moons. But there is no way they could support life. Just imagine donning your bikini for some Saturnic summer sun with the temperature a balmy minus 201° Celsius, that's minus 330° Fahrenheit. We have to solve our population problems here on earth. And we may already be too late!"

"The world has been following your communiqués and there are many questions about your strong advocacy for licensing parents to have children as the only hope for humanity."

"When I left my beloved country on October 12, 1999 it was not significant that my voyage began on Columbus Day. What was significant was that it was the day that the six billionth baby was born on our planet. In Sarajevo, Bosnia. Kofi Anan, the Secretary General of the United Nations made the trip to the Balkans to celebrate, with trepidation. And the World Health Organization acknowledged it, with fear for the future. Planned Parenthood shuddered with anxiety and a renewed sense of panic. And the irreverently intelligent cried for the future of their children.

"Then 12 years later, on October 31, 2011 the seven billionth soul arrived—this time in the Philippines. And here in 2025 we are due any day for the eight billionth.

"The overpopulation of the earth with its attendant problems of insufficient clean air and water, of loss of soil and oxygen producing trees, the population induced weather changes, the skyrocketing costs of food and energy, and the rapid accumulation of waste made me eager to begin my voyage into the deepest regions of the solar system searching for a hospitable settlement site for those who wished to escape the ecological disaster which humankind has unthinkingly brought upon itself.

"Over half of the world's population now live in cities. This has concentrated the poverty, the number of slums, and increased violence.(1a) In five years, by 2030, five billion will live in the cities. Here in California our population will double to 60 million people in the first half of this century. Most of this growth occurs because of births in the cities, not because of migration. And few governments can provide clean water, sanitation and adequate housing, let alone education and health benefits for the poor.

"There are no easy solutions to the problems created by the continuous increases in the population. On the one hand some politicians and businessmen think that such increases are necessary. Younger workers must pay for the older citizens who retire earlier and live longer—and with those longer retirements more workers are necessary to pay for them because lawmakers did not require workers to contribute enough of their salaries to pay for their own retirements. Business, of course, is always looking to increase its consumer base. The obvious solution for this problem is to increase the death rate. But those of us who are alive don't like that option. But you remember what the English philosopher Francis Bacon said, 'He that will not apply new remedies must expect new evils, for time is the greatest innovator.'"

"And George Orwell said 'To see what is in front of one's nose needs a constant struggle.' Maybe that's why we don't hear much about the crisis in overpopulation. We just hear daily about the things it causes-- like climate change, immigration problems, starvation, under-nutrition, the lack of adequate universal education, terrorism and unemployment, without acknowledging the obvious. Why?

"You mentioned business. It reminds us of what Confucius said, 'The superior man understands what is right; the inferior man understands what will sell.' But what solutions do you have in mind?"

"There is no single solution to the problems released by Pandora's population box. To solve the problem of longer life spans and early retirements we just have to increase the length of the working life before we can allow one to retire. But there's a lot more to the problem than just providing old age benefits. If it isn't too late, we can follow the lead of those few countries that have licensed parents to have children. (Books 3, 5, 7, 9, 11) It seems that it is a major hope to bring the world back into ecological balance and guarantee that each child born will have every possibility to develop physically, mentally and emotionally and to achieve his or her greatest potential in a loving family. Only then can we reach the utopian goal that has been the dream of the philosophers and saints who have preceded us. Too many of us live with the hope that somebody else will do it. This guarantees that it won't be done. We should heed Ben Franklin's advice that 'You may delay but time will not.' I know that my ideas, and those of a few of us who have seriously considered reducing population—and making it better through more effective parenting—run counter to the tenets of some religions, most businesses and the anchors of tradition that hamstring our lawmakers. But this challenge is nothing new. As Voltaire warned us "It is dangerous to be right in matters on which the established authorities are wrong."

"But I want to see how religions that are often violently competitive live in peace when I visit Muchinju. (Book 13) I want to look at how the United Colonies (Book 9) seem to have perverted the concepts of justice and democracy which have led them away from any utopian goals. I want to examine some countries that seem to be moving towards a utopia and some countries that seem to be moving away from such a goal. Are we to wait until God solves the problem or should we assume that God wants us to solve our own problems with our minds—that many believe are in the image of God. I don't think that God wants us to wait for another flood or another Sodom. But it seems like the huge majority of people in the world want to leave their futures to the gods. The live with hope—and have faith that their hopes will come true.

"When you are forced to find an answer to a major problem, it is practically guaranteed that you won't like the answer—but not following the dictates of the answer will only lead to greater and more disastrous problems. It is a sad fact that the huge majority of us live only in the NOW. The comfort of the 'NOW' blinds us to our probable future.

"Our fairytale outlook believes: 'There will never be another war. There will never be another terrorist attack. No one I know will every be robbed, killed or go bankrupt.' We content ourselves with hope and faith while the realities of our nearly universal selfishness and ignorance continue to repeat the lessons of history. Will we follow that tiny minority who clearly see beyond today. Do we have the courage to make a better world for our progeny?

THE GOOD LIFE

"It's not just a question of reducing population, but of eliminating misery and increasing the 'the good life.' Some people ask why some should be so poor while others are so rich. Did you know that the thousand richest people have more money than the two and a half million poorest people? Some ask for a more equitable distribution of the wealth—as Karl Marx suggested. The problem is that there isn't as much money in the world as it appears.

When I left, the world's population of 6 billion had a world gross product of 21 trillion dollars annually. If all of the wealth produced in a year were distributed equally it would have left about $3500 for every person. That would be about the same as the average income in Poland or Venezuela but would have been considerably less than the poorest American state, Mississippi, with an average per capita income of $18,000 or rich Connecticut with an average income of $36,000. Of course countries such as Mozambique with its $94 per year income or India with $400 would have been much better off. But then by halfway through my trip the Indian economic miracle had increased by tenfold the Indian per capita income.

"By 2015 the world's gross product had increased to $73 trillion which averaged out to $14,000 per person. Connecticut had increased to an average of $55,000 per person and Mississippi to $29,000. Poland had increased to $24,000, India to $5,400 and Mozambique to 1100 and Mali with $800.. Half of the world's nations have per person incomes of under $10,000

"Still there are more than a billion people living on less than $300 per year. With over a billion people being chronically malnourished or dying from starvation, we have a long way to go to increase the standard of living for most of our human brothers and sisters. Then there are the problems of food costs that are emptying the rice bowls of the impoverished.

"There are a couple of problems however. In a democratic world would the people of Connecticut vote for reducing their incomes by 80 to 90%. Another factor is that if the money were taken out of the hands of the governments and industries there would be no money for development, unless the recipients of the $3,500 or $10,000 either decided to give some money to the government for development or decided to invest in the stock market. And how many stock brokers will have the train fare to make their daily commute from Connecticut to New York while earning only $3,500 a year?

"If our life values were in our heads and our hearts rather than in our wallets perhaps we wouldn't mind sharing everything. But having the rich nations adopt the collective generosity of the Salvation Army, Mother Theresa, Albert Schweitzer—or even Robin Hood—is a bit too much to expect when the media tell us that more is better, and keeping is better than giving.

"When I left for outer space many of the 'haves' lived in apparent luxury, while the "have-nots" lived hungry, in filth and squalor. Today, to my amazement, some of the former prosperous nations are poorer while some of the former third world nations have gained great economic advantages. The keys to both paths have been the approaches each country has taken to control or foster their national birth rates. The most startling and yet enlightening changes have occurred through various methods of decreasing populations. Especially for those countries that are now licensing parenting.

"And what about health care. Socialized medicine sounded like a good idea. The British National Health Service has over a million people waiting for hospital admission. While its stated objective is to have no one waiting more than 6 months for an operation nor more than 3 months for an outpatient surgery appointment, those dreams become more remote as the population increases—and ages. Even in rich Norway, a country with no national debt and a huge oil income, the main hospital of its capital city finds people bedded in the halls, set off from the passers-by by screens. And with the exception of the newer additions, few rooms have televisions to help patients while away the painful hours. Operations, if not emergencies, are often scheduled rather far in the future, but if the Norwegian surgeons don't get around to you, you will probably be sent to another country for the surgery.

THE NOT SO GOOD LIFE FOR TOO MANY CHILDREN

"But the major problems I see relate to a large part of the world's children. Perhaps I am a romantic, but when I hear of infants being raped in Africa, I cry. Whether it is the superstition that sex with a virgin will cure one's AIDS or whether it is merely a sexual attack by a deranged coward—it should not happen. South Africa has the highest AIDS rate in the world. By 2025 AIDS had killed over 40 million Africans. The number of children orphaned by HIV is an international tragedy.

"And what of the many thousands of children, both boys and girls, who are the unwilling participants in the child sex trade—pawns of the pedophiles in hotel rooms or in the available pornographic media. No mature adult could bring himself to think or do such unseemly acts. Yet there are many supposedly upright citizens who revel in this sickly game. Should any child be subjected to the cruelty of such sadistic mentally ill adults? Then there are numerous societies that allow slavery of one sort or another, such as the Haitian children whose parents farm them out on that anti-slavery island, or the African children who are sold outright as slaves.

"Just look at Cambodia as an example of how HIV/AIDS has cursed the population of children. While over 150,000 orphans of AIDS afflicted parents will test positive for the disease, another 100,000 AIDS orphaned children will not test positive. What kind of a life is it when the parents have died and there are no orphanages to take in these waifs? Even if this poor country could build and staff one orphanage a day it could not take care of the avalanche of parentless children.

"And what about the children of parents in war-torn countries. The Syrian revolution began in the spring of 2011. With the great exodus in 2015 and 2016—why were there so many children under five? What were their parents thinking when they conceived them?

What about children born to drug addicted parents? What about children born into poverty where they will not get adequate nutrition. What about children born to parents who are not concerned with education?

"But it is not only the poor children who are endangered by overpopulation. As advanced countries expand their atomic power generating capabilities they build the nuclear targets for suicidal terrorist fanatics to attack. Rather than blowing up a 12 passenger bus or a high rise building, the nuclear fallout of a blown reactor can kill or maim millions—millions of young and old, good and bad, religious and non-religious. And what about the certainty that unloved children will get their hands on guns, bombs, biological or chemical weapons?

"Look at the 'crack' and alcohol syndrome children of addicted parents. Rich or poor, child abuse is a continual reminder of the plight of unwanted children.

"You may be familiar with the U.S. Center for Disease Control study in 2008. In studying 900,000 infants during their first year of life they found that one in 43 infants suffered serious abuse or neglect, a third of them during their first week of life. And one in 180 were killed. The physical abuse included beating, kicking, biting, burning and shaking; neglect included abandonment, maternal drug use or failing to meet basic needs like housing, food and clothing. The results were similar to a Canadian study.

"To avoid this cruelty should prospective parents be required to take a course in infant care in order to be licensed? Or do you think this cruelty to infants should be allowed to continue? Or possibly the drug addicted parents found in the study should not have been allowed to parent until they were clean? Should society do something to save that one in 180 who was born then killed? Children have been abused so much throughout history and throughout the present day world. I don't think it's right. I think something should be done about it. The only solution I can come up with is some kind of educational and licensing program for parents.

"Then there are the centuries-old traditions of marrying children. While it is often against the law, it is tradition. Mali and Bangladesh are among the worst offenders. The girls are deprived of an opportunity for education and the chance to make their own life choices.

"I am thoroughly convinced that parents must be capable of loving. This is a not common trait. We will learn more about this later (Book 6), but I am convinced that it is equally necessary to our survival—just as population reduction is.

OLDER NATURAL METHODS OF POPULATION CONTROL

"It all relates to too many people and to too few good parents. The older methods that have historically controlled population have been reduced. Wars are now so horrible that countries now occasionally try to avoid them. Infanticide is becoming less and less common. Legal abortion, while much safer today than in the past and safer than childbirth, often has strong antagonists. Famines still come and go but don't kill enough people to make much of a difference to the exploding population. A million deaths here or there doesn't dent the billions who roam our overcrowded home. And the advances of medicine have increased life-spans by eliminating or reducing the microbial scourges of the past, such as smallpox. And while AIDS has eliminated a large number of the population, it still hasn't taken the comparable toll that the Black Death did in Europe centuries ago.

"Still, disease and famine have been only temporary respites in the damming of the timeless flow of the geometrical increases in people's progeny. Laws and customs have to be changed. We need more than natural disasters to cope with the calamity that is already here. But there aren't enough earthquakes and tsunamis so we need intelligent action and we need it now.

"Population control is not a novel approach in either the animal or the human kingdoms. Lemmings take their fatal leaps to oblivion. Humans have practiced contraception, abortion, infanticide and suicide for millennia. Whether it was the Spartans of ancient Greece exposing their babies on the hill letting the elements determine which were the strong and which should die, or the African tribes that take the newborn of every young father into the jungle to be eaten by the animals.

"More recently we Americans have opted for unlimited firearm ownership. This allows gang members to kill each other, and for some school children to be relieved of the drudgery of schoolwork and settle into the carefree life in a grave. It allows for lawmakers, teachers and police to be killed. Guns are responsible for 20,000 suicides and over 10,000 homicides each year. Then opiate overdoses kill another 20,000. Over the years about 1.4 million Americans have died in wars, but only 6,000 or so were killed in the recent Mideast wars. Of course about 500,000 Iraqis have died from all the military violence since 2000. So America is trying to control population. I just think there is a better way—a peaceful way, a healthy way.

"Recently I have noticed that modern smartphones seem to hold more interest for people than does conversation. It appears that the digital intelligence of these hand-held devices is more fascinating than any human can be. These phones may be the most effective contraceptive we have yet devised!

"Other societies, particularly in Africa, allow the emigration of their excess population to Europe, where many will be drowned in the Mediterranean when their boats capsize. And, of course, there are the traditionally human methods of warfare and terrorism that reduce population a little bit—maybe only a million or two men, women and children, but at least that is a start! It's horrible! But we don't seem to be ready to treat the problem intelligently.

FROM THE PAST AND INTO THE FUTURE

"In the period starting a few years before I left and continuing during the twenty-five years of my voyage, many nations had intelligently come to grips with their major problem and had—through intimidation and reward, through law and ideal, and through education and science—begun to slow the raging river of ever increasing births and to turn back the tide before humanity was wiped out by its own reproductive thoughtlessness. "It is not as if the creative handling of one's population is new. In the voyage of Gulliver the First he encountered the Houynmnnms, those very intelligent equine-like creatures who limited every family to two children, one male and one female. They also had worked to select the breeding so that their nation could continue its high level of existence. They even traded children among families so that a better balance could be achieved for their race and their nation. And now there are some signs that such intelligence occasionally works on our planet.

"I hope that I will learn something on my planned visits around the world, then I'll be able to actively advocate for the plans that seem to be essential for the intelligent and joyous survival of the human race.

THE OVERPOPULATION PROBLEM HAS NO POSITIVE SOLUTIONS

"It took over 50,000 years for the Earth's population to reach one billion people. That was as recently as 1804. In 123 years, in 1927, it added its next billion. Then in only 33 years, in 1960, it reached 3 billion. In only 14 more years there was another billion. It reached five billion in 1987, just 13 years, then 12 more years to reach 6 billion. But then things started to slow a bit. It took a whopping 14 years to reach 7 billion, and in 2025 we are at over 8 billion.

"I have heard academic projections of America having a billion people in 80 years and India reaching 2 billion in 60 years.(1aa) I don't believe it will be that bad, but there are warnings that the infrastructures of the countries must be upgraded beginning now. There seems to be no end to the dire projections of world overpopulation. And nobody suggests limiting the population, only providing for it—but we can't provide for those we have now.

"Treating AIDS victims with anti-retroviral drugs has reduced the number of expected deaths by over 30 million. This keeps the victims reproducing longer. Conquering other diseases also extends life spans and enlarges reproductive windows. Poor countries like Afghanistan, Burundi, Congo, Liberia, Niger, East Timor and Uganda are projected to triple their populations by mid-century. Thank goodness for the nearly 50 countries that are reducing their native populations. Countries like Japan, Germany, Italy and South Korea would lose population if they didn't take in immigrants from poorer countries.

"In the 1990's it began to become evident to the more economically advanced countries of the western world that several factors were making it impossible to care for their citizens from cradle to grave. Earlier retirement in many countries opened jobs for younger workers—who paid the taxes necessary for the pensions of their elders. Longer life spans aided by advances in medical science and governmental or private health plans increased the need for more tax money to fund the health needs of those retirees. Jobs became more scarce as machines did the work of the unskilled and some of the skilled workers. Machines cut the wheat, picked the grapes, and built the cars and houses.

"Even skilled workers were needed less. Computers replaced accountants and many researchers. They calculated complicated medical operations while robots performed them.

Were it not for the aging populations with their increased illnesses, many doctors and nurses would have been societally superfluous. The gap between the needed high tech jobs and the traditional jobs is widening. Cars and trucks drive themselves. Robots cook, teach and clean houses. Lasers perform surgical operations. Solar energy lights our homes, propels our car and trucks and reduces our need for oil and coal. Consequently coal miner, oil workers and the ships and trains necessary to move the fuels are drastically reduced.

"Fewer people were needed to do the work of the advanced societies, but even though the birth rates per woman had fallen in most advanced countries, the longer lived citizenry more than made up for it in the burgeoning population.

"It seems that each modern decade has its special problems. The 1940s required the surrender of the German and Japanese aggressors. The 50s were quiet, but the times pushed the productive citizens toward more monetary goals while the taxes rose to take care of the education of the war babies. The 60s saw an increase in the cold war between the East and the West as it ushered in the self-centered times of the hippies—and sex and drugs became major avenues towards reducing the psychic pain of the earlier decades. The 70s recognized the problems of pollutions and the rape of the environment. Since the 80s the upheavals of Communist governments in the East allowed the western people to rest a little easier but the violent fanaticism of religious zealots endangered many countries. Crime families disrupted the cities and youth gangs terrorized neighborhoods. The 21st century began with violent selfishness, nurtured by Hollywood and under-educated imams, bringing out the worst in human emotions and behaviors.

"It became more evident that the major cause of our greatest earthly problems was rooted in our excess of population. But more than just too many people, there were too many unloved people—people born without the expected parental legacies of tenderness and caring. The poorest children among us were starved for food, but so often the children of the rich were starved for love and humanity—in an unethical uncaring society. It was evident that we not only had to reduce the gross numbers of babies being born, but we had to do our best to make certain that those who were born had the opportunity to grow into functional, loving, humanitarian citizens of the world.

"But more, the modern level of technology requires a more intelligent citizen to provide for the needs of the world's society. Shades of Hitler? No, because we have to recognize that intelligent and moral people come in every color and in every religious persuasion. Hitler was looking for perfection in only a small part of humanity—his Aryan ideal. So the ingredients in any eugenic approach to improving our collective lot would obviously come from every corner of our globe and every segment of humanity.

"In today's society there is no longer a need for chambermaids. Hotel rooms, just as private houses, clean themselves electro-magnetically at the touch of a button. Taxis and trucks drive themselves. Robots prepare the meals that the few executive chefs plan and input into their computers. Modern society does not need the peasant-slaves required in the Middle Ages to till the soil and construct the cathedrals. It needs only highly skilled architects to plan those cathedrals. It needs the truly creative artists, the master musicians, the computer engineering geniuses—and it needs thinkers to help put it all together. But the common women and men, the blue collar workers are extremely worried. They think the government should provide for them, to place them in jobs they can perform. But the jobs they could perform have gone the way of the village blacksmith and the railroad engine firemen who shoveled coal into the bellies of the puffer bellied steam engines. Intelligent people with high level educations are needed as technology fuels economic globalization. Housing prices have gone through the roof in London, San Francisco and many other cities. Only the very highly paid can afford them. There is a good chance that this will ferment revolutions as the have-nots want equality, But the have-nots have not: education, money or power. What they often do have, however, is large families, anger, and a hope that God will provide.

"If Nietzsche were alive today he might say "I told you so." Plato might see his

Republic unfolding with human intelligence as its soul. And Aristotle would marvel that a just society might really be possible.

"Well Chet, you know that the major purpose of my voyage was to find planets or moons that we could inhabit. I found none. Years ago informed researcher suggested that the maximum number of people that the planet could support was about 2 billion. How do we handle the plethora of people and how do we develop a universal good life with no poverty, no wars, no ecological problems.

"A few people are trying to educate the literate people about the problems. I have to join the fray If people merely hope that the problems of overpopulation, global warming and unloved children will somehow just go away—it will never happen. Merely hoping or wishing that the problems will go away will guarantee that nothing will happen. Remember that Ben Franklin said that 'He who lives on hope will die fasting' because 'You may delay but time will not.'

"You well know that the idea of controlling population is not new. My ancestor's biographer, the Reverend Jonathan Swift, made "a modest proposal" in the early 1700s. His idea was to prevent the children of the poor people of Ireland from being a burden to their parents or their country. He suggested that eating the little rascals would be a double blessing—healthy protein for the adults and fewer waifs on the streets. It would keep their mothers from begging for food for them and allow the ladies to work at more appropriate jobs."

"But Commander, as you know Swift was a satirist and wrote his essay with his Irish tongue in cheek, not honestly advocating a baby's thigh in his teeth!"

"Yes it was satire, but he was honestly concerned with the lack of care of the poor by the landowners and administrators. And don't we have the same thing today? Starving and diseased babies in the Third World countries and so many unloved children in the rest of the world. I am firmly convinced that it is every child's birthright to have food, safety, education and a loving family and society to give every child the physical and mental nutrients to make his or her life worthwhile. As Martin Luther King said 'There is scarcely anything more tragic in human life than a child who is not wanted.'

"I plan to visit some of those countries that have licensed parents, and some that haven't, and see what possibilities there are for reducing the total population and what can be done to guarantee life, liberty and the pursuit of happiness to every baby born into our world. They deserve no less.

"I realize that to reduce population, and especially the idea of licensing parents, not only goes against the traditions of the human race but it is definitely a politically incorrect idea. This is especially true in countries that call themselves religious or democratic because either God told us to have a bunch of babies or because our ideas of liberty include the freedom to not only have as many babies as we want but also, in many countries, the idea that the government should provide for them. Then we have the idea of some, especially in the U.S., that allowing for abortion is a politically incorrect action.

"But the ideas of which causes or actions are politically correct changes. The right, even the necessity, to own slaves was accepted when our Constitution was written, then less than a century later it was illegal and generally frowned upon. The idea of the God approved practice that women should be the homemakers and subject to their husbands has given way to having more women than men in college and the right for women to succeed in business and politics. The older politically correct idea that Jews and Asians should be kept in lowly places has given way to the reality that Jews, Chinese and Japanese are outperforming their Anglo-Christian counterparts particularly in the business and medical fields. So the ideas of the traditionalists and the idealists often change with time. But none of these threats has required a sudden reversal of tradition in order to save the race. Science affirms our common sense-- that millions of people are dying from starvation and diseases, that people have caused our global warming, that people who shouldn't have been born are murdering and raping innocents, and that the world can be a better place."

"Thank you commander. I recently saw a British television program that looked at the ecological footprint that each person born there causes. I remember only a few examples. The average Brit drinks over 2400 gallons of milk in his lifetime. He eats four cows, 21 lambs, fifteen pigs, and 1200 chickens and over 13,000 eggs. Each of the animals eats grain that could feed many starving people and each is producing methane through their flatulent farting. The methane produced is the second biggest problem in global warming. But if we could capture the methane given off by one cow in one year it would provide the power of 50 gallons of gasoline. And of course some people have powered their cars with cow and chicken manure for years.

"But back to the needs of that one Brit. He will eat over 5,000 apples and over 10,000 carrots. The amount of plastic and paper used to package the food he eats will total 8 ½ tons of garbage. The newspapers he reads will add another two tons of waste. He will produce 2,400 tons of feces and will need over 4,000 rolls of toilet paper to wipe himself. How many trees will he use to produce the paper he uses? He will buy 8.5 cars and will use 135,000 liters of gasoline to power them. So that one little bouncing bundle of British joy is a disaster for the planet.

"The more facts that are registered by my overloaded brain, the more I agree with your concerns. I certainly wish you luck. I'll help where I can. With problems like we have it is certainly a mistake to do nothing if I can do only a little. And if we can do more than a little, we must. Hope is useless without goal directed effort."

A MORE IN-DEPTH LOOK AT THE PROBLEMS

During the week that followed, Chet dutifully broadcast the weekly briefings sent by NASA. There were the somewhat detailed experiences of Commander Gulliver on each planet. There were the reports on the analyses of the soil, temperature and atmosphere. But there was nothing about the commander's concerns with overpopulation or parent licensing. And of course there were the self-congratulatory hosannas for the project and the government's funding of it. So Chet patiently waited for the end of the debriefings so that he could get the real story—the story that would shock and excite his audience. Finally on Friday afternoon he got his chance. Commander Gulliver appeared at the concluding news conference. The commander fielded a number of questions from the media. Even Chet asked about Saturn's rings, but he didn't want to ask about the real story of what Gulliver saw as the best solutions to the problem. Those were to be his scoop. As the press conference ended, Chet moved to the exit doorway to catch the hero as he made toward the door that opened into his new world, the world he had left behind twenty-five years earlier, a world more ensnarled with problems than Loki could have dreamed. Chet had to wait several minutes for the Commander to move through the swarm of newsmen. As the entourage ebbed toward the exit he found his chance to make his connection.

"Commander, now that your debriefing is finished and you have had a few days to relax, do you have some time for a more in-depth interview?"

"Sure, but can we do it at my home in Malibou Lake? I want to enjoy the unencumbered feeling that I missed in my space capsule and the four walls of these offices that have confined me the last few days. I'd like to breathe some fresh air."

"How about Tuesday at 10."

"Great, come for breakfast. We can sit on the deck and visit for a couple of hours."

"I'll be there."

Lemuel spent the weekend relaxing, seeing old friends, swimming in the lake and even took a few swings on the long thick rope that hung from the giant oak on the island. Just like when he was young! Climb up a few feet to the first big branch, grab the rope, swing out over the water and do a one and a half into the lake. Being free of the space suit and the encumbering cabin made him feel like a kid again.

He swam over to McLaughlin's dock and went for a sail with Dave Mac in his Malibou class tall mast sailboat. Dave invited him to race in the weekly three lap trip, down to the dam, back to the island then west around the buoy.

He was prepared for the weekly summer race on Sunday. It had been a long time since he'd raced and the light summer breeze barely coaxed the boats along. Thirteen boats were entered today. McLaughlin and Gulliver placed a mediocre seventh. Not like the old days when they usually won.

A neighborhood bar-b-que was held in his honor at the club. So many old friends and so little time to share with them. By 2 AM he had to head up the hill to the home his father had built in the 60s. What memories! He had lived there often during the summers while in high school and college, as well as during his early bachelor years. What a great retreat. After teaching and coaching during the school year and taking courses for his Ph.D is astrophysics at UCLA, then lifeguarding everywhere from Dockweiler to Zuma, he needed a place to unwind. With the tennis court next to the house, the Universal Gym downstairs and the lake a quarter mile away it had everything to keep his body fit to match his sound and active mind.

Nights were magic. Sitting on the expansive redwood deck he looked up at a heaven dotted with a million microscopic suns and the planets he had so recently visited. It was like being in the planetarium at the Griffith Observatory, his favorite place in LA.

Like his father before him, he was entranced by the sparkling quilt of lights that covered the sleeping city. On clear windy days he would cut his college classes and drive to the Griffith Observatory, on the south slope of Mt. Hollywood, to admire his city. From downtown to Santa Monica, from Glendale to the harbor, out past Hollywood over Palos Verdes to Catalina Island, what a view! Being up high, even though seeing only a small patch of the globe, invigorated his mind. Then at night he would eagerly await the planetarium show.

The planetarium was perched in the middle of the 75 foot diameter white plaster dome.

Then the lights dimmed to the strains of Beethoven and the blackened dome metamorphed into a crystal Sahara sky as the planetarium shot the images of 9000 stars overhead. Then came the planets and the moon. The clear celestial fantasy, an unknown phenomenon to those who live in lighted smoggy cities, brought gasps of wonder from the viewers in the circular theater. Probably only the Bedouins and Eskimos find this natural source of ecstasy in their daily lives.

Then came a famous planetarium show—'The Constellations'. 'A Trip to Mars', 'The Star of Bethlehem' and probably a hundred more. Lemuel had used it as his favorite destination for his dates with girlfriends both in high school and college. It was not only inexpensive, but it charged his imagination. It charged it enough to push him into the pursuit of a doctorate in astrophysics and astronaut training with NASA. And eventually to pursuing the passion of his dreams, the twenty-five year tour exploring the heavens.

Just like the carefree days before the voyage, he filled his days with friends, exercise, sleep and relaxation. Monday finally faded to Tuesday morning and there was Chet's red Porsche pulling up outside his bedroom. He jumped into his blue UCLA shorts and hustled to the door. Chet grabbed his recorder and notepad and walked to the steps. He looked a bit different, having doffed his newsman's uniform of coat and tie for a sporty golfer's outfit—a short sleeved autumn tan and light green striped shirt with matching green Sans-a-Belt slacks. He had the biceps of a gymnast, something hidden from his TV audience by his mandatory '6 o'clock News' suit coat and tie. As all anchormen, he was handsome. Mid-fifties, full head of graying brown hair and a smile that put everyone at ease, no wonder his program had been ranked number one for years. Even if he just sat and smiled he'd have all the women in the nation gawking. But he consistently got the inside stories that escaped his competition. Nine Emmy's in a row for the best news program.

"Well Chet, you made it to my hideaway, eh?"

"Yes commander, what a view!"

"Let me walk you around the deck and point out a few things. You know, this area was developed by some early film stars as a getaway in the 1920s. Clark Gable and C.B. deMille were among the original owners here. My dad almost bought Gable's old hunting lodge. It's on the other side of that ridge. But he bought this mountain top and built the house himself. Can you see that road beyond the white bridge on the far end of the lake?"

"Ya."

"Up to the right of that you can see the intersection with Mulholland Drive. Just to the right is Ronald Reagan's old ranch. He used to jump his horses right there. But he sold it to Twentieth Century Fox as part of their movie ranch. The ranch extends about four miles east to Malibu Canyon Road. Twentieth sold it to the state, so it is now the Malibu Creek State Park. Malibu Creek comes into the lake up there beyond that white bridge, then at the south end of the lake, that is below the house across the street, there is a dam that creates the lake. The overflow from the dam continues as Malibu Creek and it flows to the ocean south—in that direction."

"Wasn't 'Mash' filmed around here?"

"Yes. The TV version was filmed about a half mile south, in that direction. The movie was filmed about a mile east of here. Is 'Mash' still in re-runs?"

"Oh ya! Probably will be forever. I think it was the best program ever on television."

"Me too. In the old days all the movie companies had lots here. See that mountain across the lake? That's the original Paramount mountain. They haven't used that figure for years but you still see it in old films. Just beyond it is a western town that has been used for years. 'Dr. Quinn' was shot there. Hundreds of films, television shows and commercials have been made in the area, on Kanan Road, on Mulholland, at the lake. They've even used my house on occasion."

"Do any film stars still live around here?"

"I've been away so long that I don't know. Charlie Sheen used to live in that house on the other mountain top. Kelsey Grammer lived down the way on Cornell. Bob Foxworth lived on this side of the lake. My next door neighbor was Strother Martin. He was the Southern prison warden in "Cool Hand Luke" who said to Paul Newman 'what we have he-ah is a fail-

22

ya ta communicate.' That is one of the most famous lines ever uttered in a film.

"The most famous actor I ever met was James Cagney. His daughter Casey lived just down the street. One Christmas afternoon I was napping in bed, resting from a long night of assembling toys, when I heard footsteps on my redwood deck. I looked out the bedroom window and there were James Cagney and Ralph Bellamy, with Casey's husband Jack. I jumped into my sweats and met them at the kitchen door. Cagney gave me an autographed copy of his autobiography, that Jack had helped him write."

"You must have hundreds of stories, having been born in LA and living here. But let's get on with the interview. Let's try to summarize your thinking from your twenty years in space."

"Certainly Chet, shoot a question or three!!"

ABOUT SPACE

"What was it like being in space? What did you think about? Didn't it get boring?"

"Probably the major feeling I had was how insignificant I am, and how we are, when you realize what infinitesimal specks we are on our planet, in our galaxy, and in our universe. But then each of us thinks of ourselves as being all-important and having infinite worth. Some of us believe that we have been placed here by a divine creator and some of us believe that we are mere bits of cosmic dust, nearly 14 billion years removed from the Big Bang. Are we only remnants of billions of evolutionary processes who are still evolving. Or are we at the end of our evolution, rapidly becoming the victims of the suicide or our species?

"Little did Edwin Hubble know, when he confirmed that the universe has been expanding since the Big Bang, that he would have a space telescope named for him and that the findings of that telescope guided me on a human's farthest voyage into the universe. While I wasn't able to even reach the outermost planet of our solar system, and certainly could not approach a planet outside of our system, the work of Hubble and his namesake telescope have been incredibly important in making this voyage possible.

"The telescope can measure the distances to 18 galaxies, some as far as 65 million light years away. Since light travels at 186,000 miles per second a light year is about 6 trillion miles. That's a long way! It's incomprehensible. It must be halfway to infinity! We are getting more information and proof of dark matter and dark energy so we are getting a better picture of the dynamics of the universe and of its beginning."

"We know the speed of light. What's the speed of dark? Couldn't resist that! By the way Commander, do you know that the U.S. national debt is over 15 trillion dollars. That's a lot of money. Even more incomprehensible than the expanse of the galaxies. Fifteen trillion dollar bills, that if laid end to end, could reach Mars and return to Earth about 1300 times."

"But that's another problem, Chet. Let's get back to the universe. Measuring the expansion of the universe it is now possible to see that the universe is almost 14 billion years old. 13.7 to be exact. We have seen 1,500 galaxies in various stages of development. Some as old as 10 billion years. And it all started from a small bit of matter, probably smaller than a teaspoonful. In about a trillionth of a second the Big Bang exploded into the seeds of our expanding universe. At least that's the thinking now!

"Since the Big Bang, millions of species have evolved and died out, usually from things beyond their control. Our species also seems to be heading to oblivion, and it's our own fault. We have used a great many of our irreplaceable natural resources and we have polluted our water, our air and even our stratosphere.

MAKING A BETTER LIFE

"Do we have even a faint hope of saving ourselves from extinction? If so can we make a better life for our species. There were a few glimmers of hope, like when I found that there was water on Enceladus, one of Saturn's moons, but to get the necessary heat to support human life would have required us to dig deeply into its crust. That, and the fact that it is only a few miles wide and takes seven years to get there, rules it out for a future home for our excess population. Maybe some day a time machine or an astral travel mechanism can be invented that would make emigration there a possibility. But that won't solve today's emergency. The fact is that the human race is approaching extinction because we are raping our Mother Earth."

"That seems rather pessimistic commander. Your voyage began with such great hope. Have you given up?"

"Not at all. I sincerely believe that we have a real hope for our future, but it can't be realized unless people can see the problems, understand their consequences and solutions, and are willing to cooperate immediately to save us from ourselves. But the solutions would require that the richer people of the world give up some advantages that they have traditionally enjoyed. They certainly must think of working more years before retiring. They need to adopt a toned down appetite for the that many people equate with the good life—like housing opulence, when a smaller dwelling would do. And probably most important, a state mandated reproductive control. This would probably only have to last for a couple of generations until the world's population came under control and people would finally recognize the increasing scarcity of Mother Nature's blessings and work to conserve what we have left. It goes without saying that we must severely reduce the negative excesses with which our so-called advanced societies have polluted the planet. As the historian Arnolds Toynbee said, 'The human race's prospects of survival were considerably better when we were defenseless against tigers than they are today when we have become defenseless against ourselves.'

"When people are too blind to see or when their vision is too narrow to focus, we have real problems in getting things done. There are none so blind as those who refuse to see. The intellectually blind stonewall any real progress because they cannot see alternatives.

Their minds are made up before the issue is even stated. Getting the ignorant to think is like leading an army or rocks. There won't be any movement.

"In spite of the fact that human history is largely a chronicle of tragedy, with wars and natural disasters killing millions upon millions, people keep thinking that things will get better even though the evidence is stacked against it in an impenetrable wall. Every scientific and historical fact shows that we cannot survive with this many people, even if we significantly reduce our opulent way of living. We can dream the impossible dream with Don Quixote, the man of La Mancha, but the dream that we can support the present world population in the style of the average Californian is not only ephemeral, its reality can never be. We may be mesmerized by a hope for our future, but death is sure if we don't skid to a stop in our population growth. Then we must quickly get it into reverse if we are to survive. It is my mission to get the people to understand the reality of impending doom if we don't change course quickly. Too many people are like the queen in Alice in Wonderland who said that sometimes she believed in six impossible things before breakfast. We have to make people believe in the possible and make the necessary changes in their national objectives and in their personal lives. We have got to do it—not just dream or talk."

"As I remember Toynbee also said, in his best psychological insight, 'A life which does not go into action is a failure.' Sounds to me like you are ready to go into action."

"Ya, that was one of his observations that got me charged up to do something. But it's not enough to just save our species. Nearly all human lives can be happier and more productive.

Ashley Montague, my favorite social thinker, and Sigmund Freud, not one of my favorites, agree that for our mental health we need the ability to love and to work. Mental health is certainly a key to happiness, but there is so much more."

"People have been warning against robbing and trashing our planet for decades and little has been done. How would you expect to make a difference Commander?"

"I would hope that my relatively high profile will get me an audience. The U2 singer Bono got a worldwide audience because he was a famous musician. Bill and Melinda Gates had notoriety because of their vast wealth and philanthropy, and the way Microsoft had changed the world. Mother Theresa gained unwanted fame through her quiet charity. I don't have the rabid following of a famous rock singer, or the reputation of a genius or a saint. I don't have the riches to make a rapid change in a society's economy or health. But I have been on the international stage through the news media daily for a number of years. And I do have the passion to help humanity if I can."

"How would you start your crusade?"

"Well, it's about the three Es—ethics, economics and education. Certainly voluntary population control has come to many countries that have a high standard of living because of the people's education and economic means. Their ethics, relative to having children, have often been based on a self-centered system of morals."

"Are you saying that recognizing our selfishness is imperative to limiting the population?"

"No, but it is important. Women who want careers may not want children. The joys of professional success may be more meaningful for some than the potential joy of having children. Most sociological and psychological studies show that childless marriages are generally happier than those with children. Of course many marriages are greatly enriched by children. "Another disadvantage of having children, for some people, is the cost of having and raising a child. For a middle class family in the United States the cost is calculated to be 150 to 450 thousand dollars plus college costs. British studies estimate child raising costs to be 60 to 250 thousand pounds to age 17. These costs obviously include food, clothing and medical care, but they probably also include pre-school expenses, a bigger home, more electricity, summer camps, a car when the child gets to high school, increased insurance costs, and a number of other expenses. These expenses hit hard at the poor, but they also impact the middle class families who are aspiring to be upwardly mobile—keeping up with the Joneses."

"So economics is a major factor in reducing family size?"

"Yes, that and the realization of the costs of children—in time and in money. If you are a middle class couple, having a child will probably preclude your taking that trip around the world, enjoying some operas in Verona or Milan, spending a week at Club Med, or relaxing after work with a good book. Many people realize that what they want out of life is more likely to be realized without children—or without a partner. But tradition is deeply ingrained in most of us. To break that tradition by being unmarried or childless will likely make us the objects of scorn by those wedded to society's traditions."

"So you are saying that selfishness is not necessarily bad?"

"No, Chet. If it makes for happier people, that is good. If it helps reduce the population, that is good. If it stops people who would not be loving parents from having children, that is positive. Having every child born being given every advantage possible is an even more important goal of mine than reducing population. We must have parents who will provide for the physical and mental needs of their offspring."

"This is where you are getting into ethics and values. What other ideas do you have in these areas?"

"I've been studying the areas of ethics, morals and values for a long time but I don't have the answers to these enduring questions of living intelligently. I have been invited to visit Kino by Professor Wang. I expect to learn more about how our value systems can be made more user friendly. Obviously today not everyone looks to religion for their values. Religions can give us a certainty that we all would like, but history is replete with religiously unethical behavior by the proponents of every belief. Catholics fought Protestants. Protestants fought each other. The Muslims fought them both and each other. History seems to be nothing more than religions and wars, and religions were the instigators in many of those wars."

"What about economics? Do you propose a leveling of wealth?"

"No. I'm definitely not a Marxist—farthest thing from it! But through education and opportunity we can give everyone a shot at intellectual and economic wealth. Education, as I see it, is the process of teaching people to think intensively and to think critically. Intelligence plus character -- that is the goal of true education. I know you have been to Royce Hall at UCLA and seen Josiah Royce's words that 'Education is learning to use the tools that the race has found to be indispensable.'

"If we use the right tools economic wealth in the world can be increased. But there still isn't enough to go around and give everyone the equivalent income of today's average American or Brit. The other day I mentioned the wealth of the world when I left. It was about $3500 per person. Now I've had a chance to update it to today in 2025. If we were to divide the total wealth of the world, estimated at 55 trillion dollars, by the approximate population of the world, somewhere around 9 billion people, if each person got an equal share it would amount to about $6,100. I would guess that several people with more than six thousand dollars would not be willing to let go of what they have that is in excess of $6,000. If you own a house worth $250,000 you will need to share it with about 30 other people. If your only possession is your $8,000 five year old Mercedes, you can keep it all for yourself, but you couldn't keep your clothes or your furniture.

"While it doesn't make any sense to play a communist Robin Hood, robbing the rich and giving to the poor, the world can do a few things to keep the money where it benefits the citizens. Just look at the uncommonly corrupt leaders in Africa who have feathered their economic nests with the wealth stolen from their nations' foreign aid gifts by the 'do good' countries. If they don't steal it outright, they own the companies that service the firms founded on foreign money—the cleaning services, the copy machine maintenance companies, the various suppliers—fear not, much of the financial fodder finds its way to the stallion in the chief's stall.

"If we equalize incomes for all the people in the world the average person from Luxemburg would have to give up about $55,000 per year. The average Norwegian and American would have to give up about $35,000 a year. Would they stand still for losing their houses because they couldn't pay the mortgages? Would they be willing to give up their sun and snow vacations? Their cars? On the other hand the people of Gaza, Somalia, Liberia and Ethiopia would increase their incomes by over 1000% if they were given $6,100 a year.

UNHAPPINESS

"No child deserves to be born to a life of drinking contaminated water, without sanitation, and with no educational opportunities. No child deserves to be born poor, to a birthright of AIDs, or should I say a 'birth-wrong'? And no child should be imprisoned in a life without opportunity.

"Politicians make us happier by reducing our taxes while spending more. They campaign on the need for more money for education, then after the election it's business as usual slopping the pork barrels.

"Religious leaders promise 'pie in the sky bye and bye.' They say God's angry with us when things go wrong, then they praise God when blessings come—whether it is good weather or a victory in a war or on the football field.

"Whether it is retirement pay increases, state run medical programs or the promise of a heavenly salvation after our retirements end—count on our leaders to give us hope today.

But are they doing anything significant for our future? In the U.S. when gasoline prices go up a bit the president promises to look into alternate energy sources. Didn't anyone think fifty years ago that there might not be an infinite supply of oil? In Europe they were paying two to three times the price in the U.S. and didn't cry nearly as much! Of course driving alone in one's Cadillac, when one might take rapid transit, is a basic right of Americans—possibly more prized than the right to free speech.

"Maybe God will provide. After all, gasoline is free once you pass through those Pearly Gates. Will God provide more forests to eat up the carbon dioxide and stop the global warming? Will God provide water to raise the rapidly falling water tables worldwide. What is God providing for the HIV orphans? Will God provide storms to sink the fishing vessels that are denuding our seas of fish? Or has God made us in His image and expects us to use our reasoning to do something about the mess that we have created for ourselves on our planet? Is He testing our intelligence and resolve to see if we can find a way out of our predicament? Is He seeing how far we can go in terms of omnipotence—actually using our power to do what is necessary?

"Are we dealing with the vengeful Being of the Old Testament times or with the forgiving Being of the more recent scriptures? Shall we be punished for what we have done to our present day Eden or are we being given the chance to make things right? Can we eliminate famine, disease, crime, wars and pollutions? I believe we can. But it will be nearly impossible—and it seems to run counter to the human nature we have developed as we have stumbled selfishly through our history."

POVERTY AND FAMINE

"Commander, do you see any real hope for homo sapiens?"

"I see lots of hope, if we can develop a real resolve. In China 100 million people have been lifted from poverty during the last 10 years. This is due in large part to their wsld policy."

"But that was only the result of a totalitarian regime's usurping the traditional freedoms of the people."

"That's true Chet. It's unfortunate that people seldom want to do voluntarily what is best for their society. Sometimes they will, sometimes they won't. Just look at the military draft. It is a totalitarian solution to what the national leaders see as essential for the society. Your choices are to serve in the army or to emigrate.

"Forcing people who want to drive to pass a licensing examination is totalitarian. Of course it is not objectionable if you don't want to drive. But even if you don't drive, if you want to walk and cross the street you will want drivers who know they should stop for you. So driver licensing is a bit of a safety advantage for the drivers and the pedestrians.

"Korea went from a third world country to a first world country in 40 years. It took some money and some discipline to do it. It also took centralized planning and action.

"On the other hand more people live in poverty in the world than was true 10 years ago. One in seven of the world's population is going hungry (1aaa) Not so much because of a lack of food as the lack of political will to get the food where it is needed.

"It was recently believed that globalization, freeing international trade, reducing tariffs and governmental subsidies and outsourcing work would reduce poverty. But population gains propel the curse of poverty faster than anyone could have projected. (2) As global warming reduces the rainfall in the food exporting nations and as the population continues to increase food shortages develop and more people die of starvation. The price of food keeps rising, even in recessions. People living on a dollar or two a day can't buy food, even if it is available. One in six people in the world is either hungry or starving. Food grants from richer countries don't buy as much food as they once did. And the grants get smaller every time a country enters a recession.

"The World Bank projected that from 1990 to 2015 320 million would be lifted above the $2 a day poverty level. They had to change their projection to about 75 million lifted from poverty in that ten year period. But in those years the population of the world increased by about 2 billion people, many in those extremely poor countries. The fact is that poverty increases as population increases. We can't thrust a hundred million babies a year into our world without negative consequences. In fact, to keep today's average person's $8,000 share of the wealth of the world constant we would have to add $800 billion dollars a year to the wealth of the world. Then we would have to assume that some of that wealth would trickle down from Wall Street and Fleet Street to the streets of Ethiopia and Gaza. But that's not how an amoral free enterprise system works.

"Additionally, because more than half of the world's population lives in cities. More crime now occurs, in part because of a lack of jobs, in part because of the violence born of frustration and anger, in part to fund the appetite for drugs whetted by the overwhelming need for emotional escape. Crimes against people generally increase because of anger. Crimes against property, such as burglary and robbery, generally increase because of financial need.

"I was impressed with the warnings of Paul Ehrlich, the Stanford biologist, when he warned of overpopulation. He wrote that the maximum population of the world was between

1.5 and 2 billion people. That's the maximum! We reached that over a hundred years ago! We are now at 9 billion. It's a problem that humans have created and it must be solved by humans."

"Commander, I've read of maximal earth population being as high as 50 billion people."

"There have been a couple of estimates made by physicists in which they calculated the amount of heat people's bodies would put out and how that 150 watts per day per body would impact the earth. Using only this measure they concluded that the Earth could handle 40 to 60 billion people. But these projections did not include global warming from human industry, food needs, industrial needs for 50 billion people, the lack of fresh water, or all of the other factors.

"It is impossible to calculate how many people the Earth can handle without first determining at what level of comfort the people should have. If people want to live at the comfort level of Western Europe or the U.S. the calculations will be quite different than if everyone is to live at the comfort level of the average person in Bangladesh. Thirty average Indians use fewer resources than one American. So what is called 'the carrying capacity' of the world or the 'ecological footprint' of an individual are essential in estimating the number of people the world can support. Would you be content being a starving woman in Darfur dodging the rapists and the murderers who will conquer you and your country? Would you change places with a mother of ten living in a tin shack in a South African township? Would you choose to live in a favela in Sao Paulo with drug gangs in control of your slum neighborhood? Or would you prefer to live in a rambling ranch style home in Carmel, an ocean view luxury apartment in Monaco, or a seaside mansion on Chios?

"Just look at the roads needed. Americans complain about their crowded roads and freeways now. To keep an equivalent number of roads for a world population of 50 billion, if the sparsely populated U.S. kept an equivalent percentage of people it would have nearly 3 billion inhabitants. Keeping the same number miles of roads per person, it would need about 36 million miles of roads. If the roads were made of asphalt we would need more oil because asphalt is a petroleum product.

"It's a matter of ecological economics. At what level of consumption shall the world's population live? If we want to live at the level of Bangladesh perhaps we could support 14 or 15 billion people. If we want to live at the consumer level of a middle class American it would be closer to one or two billion people. But there are other considerations in determining a maximal population. We must consider how much of the society's consumption is in renewable resources, like fresh water and food. Then how much is in non-renewable sources, like petroleum and copper. Then what are the lingering negative effects of the technology, such as the disposal of nuclear and non-nuclear waste, the production of carbon dioxide and methane, and the effects of other pollutants on the air and water.

"The ecological footprint may be said to indicate how many acres or hectares it takes to support a person. A hectare is ten thousand square meters or almost two and a half acres. The Earth has about eleven billion hectares, or 27 billion acres of biologically useful area. The biologically useful area is 22% water, 14% crop land, a third forests, a little less than a third of grazing land. About 2% of the land has been built on for cities and other building. The average hectare use is about two hectares, or five acres, per person.

"Perhaps the earth could handle 15 billion people if we regressed 3000 years in terms of housing, transportation and food. We would have to keep the farming capacity that we have today with our present yield per acre. But today's farming requires huge fields that would be largely occupied by those 15 billion people. Of course we can build vertical farms that use hydroponics. Today's farms require large machines powered by oil. They require great amounts of water, which would have to be produced expensively by desalinization. We would need many more times the amount of pesticides and fertilizers than we use today. No one could drive a car because of the lack of oil and the air pollution. We couldn't all burn wood fires for cooking and heating, because there wouldn't be enough wood and the fires of 15 billion people would pollute the air and increase the carbon dioxide levels. And then, common sense tells you that the advanced living standards of many counties today cannot be voluntarily ended.

DEATH AND DISEASE

"Ten million children are dying each year from disease and starvation. Children are born to AIDS infected parents in Africa, India, China and in most other parts of the world. Is this what you want for your grandchildren? The deaths may help to curb the population explosion but is it worth the sadness for the children? As great as the disease problem may be, with influenzas, AIDS, malaria, ebola, cholera, drug resistant tuberculosis and all the other afflictions of humans, it's not enough to stop the planet's strangulation death by the human python.

"Do you remember the study done in the late 1960s by John Calhoun? (3) In 1968 he put four pair of mice in a 10 foot by 10 foot enclosure. He provided them with a perfect air conditioned environment with plenty of food and water. By the time the population reached 150 all the good places to live and the major social roles were taken. Shortly after this population mark had been reached, mothers began chasing their babies from their nests—before trust could be established. Dominant males got tired of protecting their territories and quit. Females became more aggressive and took over the dominant roles. The males crowded together. Homosexuality increased. By the time the population reached 2200, in 1970, mating stopped and by January of 1973 the last mouse died. He did similar studies with rats. Might our human population do this? Or might we, like the lemmings, follow each other off a cliff? Is the ultimate control of population in our mammalian genes?"

NATURAL DISASTERS

"Commander, even if we don't make any adjustments, nature will control population through famine, disease, war and terrorist uprisings, major volcanic eruptions, tsunamis, and so forth."

"But it would take a heck of a natural disaster to significantly reduce the human race. The famous eruption of Vesuvius in 79 AD only buried a few thousand people under the lava at Herculeneum and the ash at Pompeii. Krakatau's eruption in Indonesia in 1883, an eruption that had worldwide effects in terms of released ash and ocean disruptions, only killed about 30 or 40 thousand people. The Southeast Asian tsunami of December 2004 killed about 240,000 people, the earthquake in Haiti in 2010 killed 200,000, but the one a month later in Chile only killed a couple hundred even though the quake was 500 times stronger than the one in Haiti.

The people in Chile were financially better off and better prepared for the natural disaster so it did not take as much of a human toll. Then there was the Myanmar cyclone of 2008 that killed over 120,000.. But the world adds 200,000 people per day, with about 350,000 births and 150,000 deaths. The earthquake in Pakistan in 2005 killed 80,000 people. But it only took eight hours to restock the earth's population. The earthquake in China in 2008 killed about the same number of people that are born in China in a day. So the most devastating natural disasters in memory just slowed the population explosion by less than a day and a half. It's hard to count on natural disasters to slow our destruction of ourselves.

"Of the ten worst storms in history, six have hit Bangladesh killing over a million people, still Bangladesh is the most densely populated large country in the world with over 1000 people per square kilometer.

"Maybe a real disaster could help slow the rape of the planet. The last eruption of the currently active volcano at Yellowstone National Park in Wyoming might make a dent. Its last eruption, two million years ago, released enough ash to cover the state of California under 6 meters of ash. We are entering a geologic era where Yellowstone should erupt again. Then there is that big quake that is overdue in California. Or maybe God will send us another great flood and let us start over with a dozen or so people!"

"Commander, I've heard that the Earth's magnetic field seems to again be shifting. This can have the effect of allowing harmful cosmic rays into our atmosphere. These rays can destroy our DNA and kill us all."

"Chet we'll never last that long. It would take many thousands of years for that to happen. We also can't count on volcanic eruptions, earthquakes and tsunamis to do what we should do if we are really homo sapiens—thinking people."

WARS, MASSACRES AND FAMINES

"What about the human inflicted catastrophes, commander? In the past we could count on wars and massacres to help control the population. Napoleon certainly did his part, being responsible for as many as 6 million dead—half from opposing armies, a quarter from his own and the rest civilians.

"Shaka, the Zulu chief claimed one to two million in his wars. About 3 million died in the Islamic slave trade and almost as many in the slave trade in the western hemisphere.

Look at the human cost of Central and South American wars with over a million killed. And the American Civil War killed 600,000. Even the little old Crimean War took a half million lives. Over four million were killed in the Congo in the wars that began in 1998, but that was only about 6% of their population so it only put a small dent in their population growth rate.

"And how about the famines? Famines in India in the late 19th century took 15 to 30 million lives, the 'potato famine' of Ireland 750,000."

"Ya Chet, but without that potato famine I wouldn't be here. My grandparents immigrated here so they wouldn't starve. Heck, if it weren't for the famine I'd probably be a priest in Galway!"

"You bring up religion, what about the religious wars and massacres: In the mid-1800s the Taiping Rebellion in China took 20 to 30 million lives as people fought for a one God theocracy—and lost. The Thuggee sect of the goddess Kali sacrificed a half million in India. Muslim rebellions in China killed another 300,000."

"Chet, let's not forget ethnic and religious cleansing. Between 100,000 and a million American Indians were killed by the good Christian invaders. In Australia 300,000 Australian aborigines were eliminated in their own land by the white settlers. And of course 6 million Jews, gypsies and other religiously or ethnically objectionable people were gassed by the Nazis.

"Just looking at the 19th century, the large and small wars, famines and uprisings killed about 54 million during the century. We could assume that these killings and starvings reduced the population at the end of that century by about 3% from what it might have been. The 20th century inhumanities also accounted for about another 3% drop in the 6 billion population. Of course because there were more people, there were more total deaths.

"Thanks to better weapons, the psychotic warlords of the last century were incredibly effective murderers. In the 20th century we're talking about 200 million or so war deaths, with Mao leading the pack at 30 to 60 million, Hitler and the Axis powers accounted for 55 million and Stalin was responsible for another 20 million.

The Islamic State, or ISIL, as well as Shabab in East Africa and Boko Haram in West Africa certainly are doing a brutal job of reducing population. It seems to be even more brutal than our American method of population control—allowing guns to just about everybody!

There must be better ways of controlling population than having uneducated religious zealots and uneducated power-hungry macho people and psychotics, killing whoever stands in their way. But since people are generally controlled by emotional rhetoric that sooths their power drives, rather than logically considering the facts, I guess we have to live with it. In the time I have left on our planet I certainly hope I can see the issues more clearly and help others along a peaceful path by using our intelligence to preserve our home."

"Didn't realize it was so many, commander. So obviously wars, revolutions, massacres and famines are not doing the job of effectively controlling our population. We need about a 70% drop in population, not a piddling 3%. So do we need bigger bombs, larger scale wars, greater levels of genocide?"

"Perhaps it's time to try a peaceful and intelligent method of doing it. But then that would hurt the economy if the world's weapons dealers had no one to sell to!"

"Commander, are you sure that with global warming and the eventual lack of water we won't have some really effective famines? Maybe they will supplement the natural disasters enough to reduce our population to manageable levels. Maybe these are more likely than doing it voluntarily."

UNEMPLOYMENT, IMMIGRATION, MENTAL ILLNESS AND CRIMINALITY

"Chet, it is more than just reducing population. It's about making the population mentally, physically and economically healthier. Just look at the number of people in prisons and mental institutions. Some of their propensities are probably genetic. To the degree that genes are responsible perhaps we can either weed the poor risks out of the reproductive population or manipulate the genes once they are born. But for the greater number of people whose poor upbringings did not develop in them sufficient self respect and the capacity to love—we should be able to reduce their percentage. In my mind it is our greatest human tragedy to have children born who are not loved and cared for, who do not have the advantages of an outstanding education. It is an international disgrace to have so much crime committed and to spend so much money on police, the judicial systems and the penal systems. Wouldn't it be nice to be able to put that money into higher education and more extensive recreation facilities?"

"I think everybody would agree with you on reducing the prison populations. A few years ago I did a TV series on crime and prisons in different parts of the world. Some, like in

Malawi are hideous. With 160 crowded into a single cell, one meal a day, polluted water, foul toilets and not knowing how many months or years before they would see a judge, it was dismal. On the other hand in Norway a prisoner might have his own TV and computer and three meals a day. They are even paid while imprisoned! I thought about doing jail time in Norway for a vacation. Of course in the States we have the highest number of inmates per capita.

"And look at the types of crimes committed. As bad as we may think America is for murders, it is way down the list when compared to Columbia and South Africa. Interpol told me that the per capita murder rate there is ten times more than in the States."

"That's my point Chet, I sure would like to find other ways than murder, war and genocide to keep the population controlled."

"There's certainly more to the crime problem than murder. You have heavily funded organized crime worldwide. South Africa has 700 well financed crime syndicates. Columbia is worse. Russia is infected. And we certainly know a bit about the Italian and Sicilian mafias from the movies. Even the welfare paradise Norway has its Yugoslav mafia. Hollywood has its Mexican mafia. Sometimes I think that the criminals run the world and if they don't run it, they sure have a big piece of the pie!"

"It is also obvious that the world society has not been able to produce enough jobs for the world's population. And it's not just about jobs it's about interesting and creative jobs. Every country has some level of unemployment, and the more populous regions seem to have even less ability to produce jobs than do the advanced countries. The search for jobs is a major reason for immigration, particularly illegal immigration. Look at the problems caused by the illegal immigration of Central Americans into the US and of Middle Easterners and Africans into Europe. When the society has too many children for the jobs it can produce it creates problems both for itself and for its neighbors.

"As long ago as September 2014 the OECD, the Organization for Cooperation for Economic Development of the developed Western countries issued a report saying that over 7% of workers would be unemployed the next year and that half of the developed world's workers had experienced pay cuts. It went on to say:

"A key lesson that policymakers and governments must draw from the findings of the OECD Employment Outlook 2014 is that in a context of weak aggregate demand and disappointing job creation in most economies, austerity policies and supply-side interventions are failing to boost growth and employment. Governments should increase public investment in infrastructure to support aggregate demand, and boost employment in the short-term while mitigating the adverse consequences of long-term unemployment.(3a)

"Even before the turn-of-the-century there were overpopulation problems. However then many people could go to advanced countries and get jobs—as taxi drivers, shopkeepers, and laborers. But as the population explodes, particularly in the Muslim countries, Africa, South America and India we get revolutions to get more jobs. But computers and robotics are replacing the former jobs and doing them better and cheaper. Self driving cars, bar codes and machines replace millions of humans.

"When jobs are not available we get young men and women joining violent groups like: ISIL, Boko Haran, Al Qaeda, al Shebab, Taliban and hundreds of others. We get Muslims killing Muslims, Muslims kidnapping Muslims, Islamists doing their best to gain control of any territory. And it is going to get worse. We see the rioting of young blacks in the US and France. They look for a cause such as police brutality then their drive for power turns to rioting and looting. We see gang rapes in India and the murdering of their victims. We see gang warfare throughout central and South America. There are too many people and not enough situations where they can feel content – – where they have control of their lives.

"People tend to believe the rationalizations that are given— there is police brutality, Western education must be eliminated, women are to be the tools of men, the Sunnis do not have the true religion, the Shia do not have the true religion, the Christians do not have the true religion. The Jews don't have the true religion— and the rationalizations go on.

It is all about having too many people, too few jobs, inadequate education and the fact that too many people hold to their mythologies and are not willing or able to look at the realities. Reducing population, requiring better parenting and providing universal education to the highest levels are essential if we are to save our world—BUT IT MAY BE TOO LATE!

Studies of animals and people show that most of us need to feel god about ourselves and we need an identifiable place in our society. It may be being an elected official. It may be siring the most children. It may be being a mother. It may be owning the cheese shop. So very often it is about what we do. So many people today have no place—no job, no status. Groups like al Queda, ISIL or any of the hundreds of Muslim terrorist groups can give a man or woman on instant status. Then the status is raised if we can be more brutal that our comrades. As population increases and jobs decrease we can expect more anti-social groups to bloom.

And they're not all Muslim. We have neo-Nazi parties, like the Aryan Brotherhood, black gangs like the Crips and Bloods, favela gangs in Brazil, and many many more.

BUILDING A BETTER WORLD

"But back to our major problem. Martin Luther King said it best when he warned that 'Unlike plagues of the dark ages or contemporary diseases we do not understand, the modern plague of overpopulation is soluble by means we have discovered and with resources we possess. What is lacking is not sufficient knowledge of the solution but universal consciousness of the gravity of the problem and education of the billions who are its victims.' He was a practical dreamer—an idealist with his feet on the ground. Too bad he's not still around, he could certainly do a better job of making people listen than I can. Because he was a man of color he could neutralize the cries of racial genocide that I will undoubtedly encounter. In fact I see it as 'geno-genesis' a rebirth of the human race, with people more likely to put the human values of love and compassion ahead of power and acquisition."

"But commander, as a liberal Protestant Dr. King would still face the ire of the protestant evangelicals, the Catholics, the Mormons and the Muslims. No matter how important an idea, there will be people opposed to it."

"But I believe that I must stand up for what is right, even if I stand alone. However I'm sure there will be lots of people who will join me. After all, what thinking person can be against saving the planet, making the future better for all, and working to give every child a loving start?"

"People opposed the ideas of Socrates, of Jesus, of Abraham, of Muhammad, of Buddha, of Jefferson, of Einstein."

"Was anybody opposed to Thomas Edison's inventions, Chet?"

"I don't think so. People only resist when their minds are shaken up, not when somebody produces things that ease their lives or entertain them. They don't want to hear about new gods, new types of government or about anything that relates to misery—their own or others."

"Before my space odyssey I did a bit of traveling. I've seen the misery of old Calcutta when the trucks picked up the thousands of bodies from the streets every morning, bodies that had been alive the day before. I've walked through parts of Soweto in fear, knowing that if it were not for my friend Winston, who was known and respected, I might be the next victim of robbery or murder. I've seen the hopeless faces of those in the cities and farms of Bangladesh. I've heard the gunfire in Beirut and the plastique bombs in Paris. I've lived in South Central LA amid the gang warfare.

"I long ago concluded that things can be better. Why the suffering of starvation deaths in Ethiopia? Why the beating of children in Beverly Hills? Why the white slave trade from Eastern Europe to the West? Why are so many thousands of Latin Americans risking death to cross the Rio Grande for a life in the U.S.?

"Chet, can you fathom the depth and width of the problem? It's beyond our comprehension.

--12 million children die before reaching their fifth birthday;

--100 million homeless children wander the streets and alleys of our world.

--250,000 children die every week from diseases and malnutrition. Millions of children are objects of sexual abuse, child pornography and the demand for child prostitutes is astronomical—and growing,

--20 million children are refugees of war and familial deaths,

--10 million children are child slaves—or work in slave-like work situations

--Millions of girls are 'missing' as a result of infanticide and neglect.

"In the USA a married couple was arrested for keeping 11 children in cages with very little food. Their adult daughter testified against them in court saying she had also been mistreated physically, emotionally and sexually.

"Doesn't it just tear your heart out? What would you be willing to do if one of those children were yours, or your children's children or a neighbor's child?

"For so many people it is often 'out of sight, out of mind.' It's a sad fact that for the great majority of us we are more concerned about a splinter in our finger than with the millions who are dying painful deaths in Africa. We are more concerned with pleasuring ourselves with what's on TV or playing a video game or buying a new car than we are aware with the brutal suffering of so many in our human family. While it may be true that few of us will be remembered in the pages of human history, there is no need for the great suffering that abounds in this world among us common people."

"I have to confess, commander, that I fall into that category. I'm thinking about seeing my grandson's soccer game, painting the kitchen, taking my wife out to dinner and a show. I just sort of assume that that's the way it is. You're making me ashamed of myself."

"Maybe with your writing and reporting you can help to bring some understanding, but if you are not really convinced it'll just be empty prose. There has to be a burning commitment."

"Well Lemuel, can I call you Lemuel?"

"Well we're getting along pretty well, guess we are on a first name basis. But I've never gone by my first name. Actually when I was about twelve my buddies started calling me Wreck, for shipwreck. It wasn't a bad name when I played football. I was a linebacker and part time fullback so the name fit. But a lot of girls didn't want to go out with a 'wreck.' But don't use 'Wreck' in your story, OK?"

"Fine. I was just thinking about how much money would be needed to reduce the Third World suffering and where we Americans spend our money. Americans spend more on their pets than on toys for their kids. The pet industry is said to be a 38 billion dollar industry in the U.S. Japan is almost as bad. What could that 38 billion do for our impoverished human brothers. Is it moral to spend serious money on massages, acupuncture or clothes for your dog? I know people who spend a lot of money burying or cremating their dogs and cats. Some even have them frozen. It's not enough to have yourself sealed in a cryonic crypt, hoping that someone in the future will find a cure for your fatal problem. But to take your poodle with you seems to be the height of neurotic insecurity. They argue that it's their money and they can spend it any way they see fit. And I would agree with that, but what kind of morality are we talking about when we can freeze Tabby or feed an African village for ten years with the same amount of money. Are all species equal? Is one individual of a lower species, like a cat, more important than a group in the higher human species? It reminds me of when a neighbor kid would feed mice to his snake. Why feed a higher level mammal to a lower level reptile?"

"These are some of the same incongruencies I keep seeing. Are some people more important than others? I certainly put my family first. And if I put them first I have to be concerned with how the problems of overpopulation are going to affect my children and theirs. And it's not like these problems are down the road, they are right here affecting us today.

"I had a couple of friends die of skin cancer. One was the legendary surfer Tommy Zahn, who my father used to lifeguard with. Too much sun and not enough protection from the ozone layer. Had they taken precautions early in their lives they would still be around today. We talk about an ounce of prevention being worth a pound of cure, but to reverse our excessive population while making parents more effective will take megatons of education and work. And it has to be done while dragging those megatons of solutions up the steep mountain of tradition and selfishness. The odds are certainly against my crusade for human survival!"

"I agree. But here's another thought. Just look at real estate prices. Do you think you'd have to pay 10 million for a house on Malibu Beach if there were only a thousand people in the world? We keep making more people but we're not making more land."

"Right Chet. My dad bought the land here for ten thousand dollars, it's now worth millions. But let's get back to the supposed topic of this interview. It's about the children of the world. There are too many people for the planet to support, too many people for their nation to support and too few parents with the ability and desire to raise physically and mentally healthy, happy, and educated children. We have to give all the children a chance at a real life. We must develop children with a purpose and children with a loving drive to make the world a better place.

"I'm driven by that ancient Native American reminder that 'We have not inherited this world from our forefathers, we have borrowed it from our children.' It's about the future children of the world. Are the politicians concerned? No! For most of them their concern is the immediate interests of their constituencies. Are business leaders concerned? No! More people in the short term is better for business. Are religious leaders concerned? No! The world needs more souls to be saved now. Only a few scientists and other academics seem to realize the catastrophe that is already here."

"Wow commander, you sound like Plato, Santa Claus and Mother Theresa rolled into one. But I doubt that you are alone in your hopes. I would certainly agree with you. But the questions are: how to do it, and can it be done? I think that the selfish nature of the great majority of people wouldn't be willing to make it happen."

"Well I'll be that small pebble that when tossed in the pond makes small ripples that reach every inch of the shore. Hopefully my ripple will join with others and we can make a wave.

"If the world could only honesty strive to follow what the UN Secretary General said when the United Nations Convention on the Rights of the Child was adopted. He said 'We have no higher priority, no prouder achievement, than our work for the rights of children!' If that is not just empty rhetoric let's get on with the most practical solutions we can find to make a better world.

"Insuring that children have a fair shot at a productive and happy life finds support in this UN Convention. Article 24, Section 2, requires that parents be informed of the 'basic knowledge of child health and nutrition, hygiene and accident prevention.' It also requires preventative health care and guidance for parents. And it mandates that parents 'shall take all effective and appropriate measures with a view to abolishing traditional practices prejudicial to the health of children.' The convention doesn't say that this should be done after the children are raised! It is implicit that these knowledges be learned by parents before the child is old enough to be negatively affected. Article 3, Section 2, notes the duties of parents.

"Articles 3, 18 and 21 all require that it is the 'best interests of the child' that are primary. Here we find repeated the requirement in most state laws that the child's interests, not the whims or wishes of a parent, are primary. Article 24 recognizes the right of the child to the enjoyment of the highest attainable potentials. And what's more—Article 4 mandates that 'States Parties shall undertake all appropriate legislative, administrative, and other measures for the implementation of the rights recognized in the present Convention.' This seems to me to sanction some types of requirements for parents if they choose to have children. I would call this licensing. Maybe you wouldn't, but the U.N. clearly calls for certain knowledges and behaviors of parents as duties and responsibilities for parenthood. I think that all countries have signed the UN Convention on the Rights of the Child. It was disappointing to me that my country was one of the last to sign on, and that was in 2002.

"Then Article 28 requires the various countries to provide for compulsory primary education, for various forms of secondary education, and for university education for those capable of handling it. Chet, maybe we ought to withdraw UN membership and economic cooperation with countries that don't take care of their children!"

"You are really into protecting the children. I would agree that no country does what it should to protect children or to educate parents. But just because the people at the UN come up with ideals for 'human rights' or 'child rights' doesn't mean that any country is going to follow those ideals. The world is still controlled from the top down and children are at the bottom. A few countries have done a pretty good job in providing educational opportunities, but I'm not aware of any trying to weed out bad parents before they conceive. But as I remember, George Bernard Shaw said almost a hundred years ago that 'Parentage is a very important profession, but no test of fitness for it is ever imposed in the interest of the children.'" (3b)

"We must find the seeds for the beginning of a better world. And I emphasize MUST, it's too late for 'should.' That's why I'm planning to visit with some wise people around the world and try to gain more knowledge about how to go about it. Certainly what needs to be done to limit our population and improve our world will ruffle a lot of religious feathers and trample the ingrained traditions that motivate most people."

"So Wreck, how are you going to try to educate those who have the power to sway people's opinion? As I see it science looks at how the universe works, religion and philosophy look at why. When a scientist tells you how to behave he is outside of his realm. When a priest tells you how the universe works he is outside of his realm—unless he is also a physicist or an astronomer. The religiously or philosophically adept people deal with the purpose of life.

"Those are the people who need convincing. The scientists already know the enormity of the problem. I don't think you can look to the politicians for salvation. In democracies politicians follow—they don't lead. If they don't follow the trends they don't get re-elected and that's the main concern for most of them."

"Chet, I think you are rapidly becoming a convert."

"You'd have to an illiterate idiot to not know about global warming, oil scarcity, air pollution, the accumulation of wastes, the scarcity of fresh water, and such, but with the exception of higher gasoline prices and higher utility bills my life hasn't changed that much. Maybe Einstein was right when he said 'Only two things are infinite, the universe and human stupidity, and I'm not sure about the former.' As long as our own lives are going well we think there is no need to be concerned about the future."

—"I was amazed when I got on the freeway yesterday. Wall to wall cars at about every hour of the day and night. That was one thing I appreciated about space travel— no congestion. Do people realize that all those cars are being driven by somebody else's babies?

"My grandfather used to tell me about the LA of the 30s, 40s and 50s. Few cars, a freeway or two, only a few houses from La Brea to the beach. No congestion around Mines Field, LA's only airfield, just Sepulveda Boulevard bordering its west side. Now it's LAX with freeways all around it and houses and industry from Malibu to San Diego.

"My dad used to tell me how his buddies would decide to go to Yosemite to camp on July third. They'd celebrate the Fourth in Yosemite Valley with just a few people. Now you have to get reservations a year ahead. That's just an example of how the good life of the past has been hampered. Certainly some things are better—frozen foods, fat free ice cream, more football on television,-- but lots of things are worse—drugs, violence, traffic, politicians!

"But this is the U.S. Just think about the underdeveloped countries, where everything is worse. They have less water, less food, more devastating genocidal wars, more rapes and murders. Overpopulation has occurred more in the underdeveloped areas of the world so they suffer more. Just look at how China began to prosper as its one child policy took effect. And as the years roll on its positive effects will be magnified.

"Today, in 2025, there are 9 billion people on earth. And it is increasing most in the undeveloped countries. Africa is expected to have over four billion people at the next turn of the century. And they already have famine problems in East Africa."

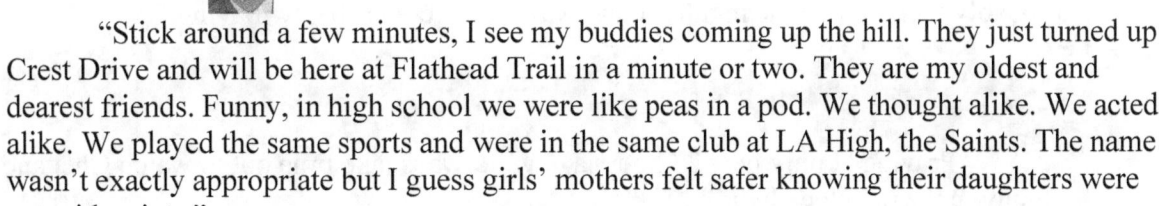

"Well commander, or should I say 'Wreck', I've taken too much of your time, I'd better be going."

"Stick around a few minutes, I see my buddies coming up the hill. They just turned up Crest Drive and will be here at Flathead Trail in a minute or two. They are my oldest and dearest friends. Funny, in high school we were like peas in a pod. We thought alike. We acted alike. We played the same sports and were in the same club at LA High, the Saints. The name wasn't exactly appropriate but I guess girls' mothers felt safer knowing their daughters were out with saints."

"OK, love to meet a part of your past."

REACTIONARY AND LIBERAL

"We're going to have a huge several month long reunion because they are going to travel the world with me on a combination fact-finding tour and vacation. I've been invited to several countries to meet with their leaders.

"I've been thinking of writing a book or working on a TV series on my voyage. I need my friends to help me understand what I will experience. Since playing high school football together in Los Angeles we have been best friends. It's funny that while at one time we were so much alike, time has etched some rather huge crevices between our world views today. We now span the political spectrum from left to right. The most left leaning is Lee. He is one of the few honest lawyers I know. Chet, is the term 'honest lawyer' an oxymoron? He's the one with the light blond hair. His gift of gab has probably swayed more than a few juries.

"The sun-tanned one just behind him, the other one with the blond hair is Frank Concannon who is our conservative. But he has always been known as Con. He was our quarterback. Always the smartest of us, Con became a multi-millionaire with some pluck and some luck. The pluck, because he was always the hardest worker of our gang, the luck because he got into the wireless communication business and sold out to a Scandinavian conglomerate. He looks fit enough to don the helmet and shoulder pads and chuck a few 60 yard passes.

"The good looking guy closing the door is Ray. He was our All City end. He got a college football scholarship to Notre Dame. They not only knocked the wildness out of him, a wildness that had so often led us astray as youths, but they put a purpose in him. This led him to become a priest, a rather reactionary priest. I guess the new term for reactionary is neo-conservative. Doesn't sound as uncivilized as "reactionary." I would never have expected Ray to duplicate the Medieval approach to religion that the Polish and German popes have been advocating. If anything, I would have expected him to follow Pope John XXIII's or Pope Francis's liberal approach. Of course I would never have expected him to become a man of the cloth. It wouldn't have surprised me to find him starring in films, coaching football, or becoming a gigolo for some rich European princess—but a priest? Of course my life couldn't have been predicted either. You know I started as a teacher and football coach. Before I was accepted into astronaut training I was the football coach at Hollywood High School. Anyway here they are.

"Guys I'd like you to meet Chet Roland from World News. Lee and Con, you've probably seen him on the nightly news. Ray, you were probably praying."

"Praying? I only pray 23 hours a day, I always take time out to watch Chet and Bugs Bunny in the 6 o'clock hour."

"With your reactionary approach to thinking I thought you only watched Robin Hood and The Flintstones!"

"Get off my back Lee or I'll start telling lawyer jokes. Or worse, I'll start rubbing it in on how bad Notre Dame beat Stanford. If you are going to go to college there is no sense going to a school without a 'top ten' football team. When you played there did you ever score?"

"We scored a lot. We just couldn't stop anybody. When Con was the quarterback at UCLA he must have thrown 20 touchdowns against us in his career. But seriously, graduating from Stanford gave me my pick of law schools. When you got out of Notre Dame did you have your pick of seminaries?"

"Sure did. And like Thomas Aquinas, I chose the Dominicans."

"Ray, what is it that has made so many powerful people look to the past for the truth?"

"Well Lee, for some reason there has been a movement towards conservatism, and often a movement to the right of conservatism to a reactionary or neo-conservative position. Rather than conserving the values that have been commonly held, some political and religious leaders are looking to values of the past which they find superior. This seems to be especially true in religious belief. Many of us think that most people have left God's word behind and have looked for the easier self-centered life. Pope John Paul the Second, Pope Benedict the Sixteenth, George W. Bush in the United States and Mahmoud Ahmadinejad in Iran, not to mention Osama bin Ladin, and then ISIK have championed earlier visions of their religions as the salvation of the world.

"Several elected African presidents have moved backward toward absolute monarchy. Drug lords, and some major companies, have cast ethics aside in an amoral laissez faire approach to making fortunes. All these are movements look back to earlier religious beliefs or back to primitive human selfishness. Many of us feel that seeking pleasure now is the big problem with society. That seems to be the reason that so many people are moving into more fundamental religions, into Islam, 'born again' evangelical Protestants and conservative Catholics like me.

"Of course you can't put religious leaders in the same camp with drug lords and unethical business or political leaders. We are going back to truth and seeking a higher level of living through God's inspiration. They are going back to the primitive aspect of savage human nature. As religious leaders we want to rise above that base level of human nature. What Con?"

"But Ray, look at your reactionary religious leaders. Bin Ladin attacked both Moslem and non-Moslem regimes that he thought were antagonistic to his beliefs. Bush attacked an Islamic country, ostensibly to rid them of a sadistic dictator and to spread democracy. But he probably actually had the economic and political goals of controlling more oil and obtaining military bases in the Mid-East. Ahmadinejad ran for president of Iran as an idealist, but once elected he quickly moved to put Iran on a path toward allegiance to the Shiite messiah, Mahdi. Some think that he believed himself to be a representative of the Mahdi and is preparing for the second coming of the 12th imam. He clearly hoped to establish a more rigid Islamic regime. Along this line he fired a number of experienced diplomats and bank directors. He wanted all the power of a Medieval religious king. While he was elected democratically, democracy was not one of his goals for his country. Chet, you seem to be bursting with a comment or question."

"Right Con. Fellas, I get the point that you are a political galaxy. But I'd like to get a better feeling of where you guys are coming from. Ray, since you have been designated as the group's resident reactionary, why do you feel that Wreck gave you that label?"

"Don't know Chet, I think I'm the most progressive of the group. What could be more progressive than trying to know God and helping people to get to heaven? But I suppose that for the last 2000 years the Christians have had this goal. Of course the Jews had that vision 3,000 years ago and the Muslims have had it for 1500 years. So by today's standards in some parts of the world I am reacting back to where we had been."

"I see Ray. I guess we all think we're progressive since we all think we are right! What about you Concannon. What makes you a conservative?"

"Well as I see it, liberty is the most important right that a government can grant. Without real freedom good things don't happen. Religions can't flourish, science can't reach its potentials for providing us knowledge, and business can't expand to bring more goods and services to more people. This means that taxes should be as low as possible while providing the means by which society can progress. And the progress of society is based on an equality of educational opportunity. Why is your face so screwed up Lee. Don't you like the idea of equality of educational opportunity?"

"Con, you are assuming that educational opportunity is a conservative idea. It's a cornerstone of our liberal agenda. I see "equality" as basic to my liberal views."

'I agree, Lee. I think that particularly in domestic issues we conservatives lean to liberty while you liberals lean towards equality. But we both agree that equal educational opportunity is essential. The difference is that we conservatives are more likely to allow people the freedom to achieve after they have experienced as much education as they like, while you liberals want to keep equalizing them. Liberty will result in longer term inequalities based on people's educations, work ethics, goals, occupations, et cetera. You are for a graduated income tax to pull back the high wage earners toward the bottom. We conservatives are more likely to want a sales tax or a value added tax, and perhaps luxury taxes on buying expensive items like furs and Ferraris."

"I see your point but I disagree with your goals. As liberals we do want more equalitarian treatment for all people. A gang member shot in a street war is just as much entitled to emergency care treatment and hospitalization as a school teacher who has had a heart attack. This means that we need higher taxes to provide more extensive medical services than you conservatives would want."

"Possibly. We disagree on a lot of things but we agree on a lot too. For example we both want effective Social Security. You liberals want it all to be handled by the government. We conservatives think that people would be more able to end up with a better retirement if they handled the same pension contributions themselves. And some people avoid the issue and just say 'have more babies' so that someone will take care of society's financial needs.

"What has happened, of course, is that the existing system, the liberal system, is supposed to give a guaranteed amount to everyone based on their years of contributions and their salaries. But tax laws have allowed a more conservative approach in which you can contribute, tax free, to your own retirement plan. So in terms of pensions we have both the conservative and the liberal ideas at work. The realities are that there are good ideas on both the left and the right and most people are a little bit liberal and a little bit conservative. Lee, you just have more of your ideas on the left side of the middle and I have more of mine on the right."

"But Con don't you think religion is a factor in how we believe?"

"I'm not particularly religious but most conservatives are, because religion like liberty, is a value that most want to conserve. But many religious ideas are quite liberal, so a majority of liberals in this country are also religious. It just happens that some people on the left, like Karl Marx, are atheists. But you have atheists on the conservative side too! You also have saints on both sides of the aisle. I think we could put Joan of Arc on the right and Mother Theresa on the left. And when they make Pope Benedict a saint we'll have a reactionary saint!"

"Well guys, I hope this upcoming trip gives us a chance for some heavy discussions. And I think we'll meet some people who will shake us up intellectually. As you know I am deeply concerned with population reduction and making a better life for all children. So that will be a major concern of mine as we travel."

"I'm with you Wreck. But how about filling us in on what you see as the background of the problem. We should start with some basic information."

POPULATION CONTROL AND REDUCTION

"Well Con, as I had mentioned to Chet, look at the way world population has increased. In all of human history it took us until 1800 to reach a billion people. Now we have 9 billion. And we are expecting it to be 10 billion in 2050. If the population continues at its current rate, by the year 2855 it has been estimated that there will be about 20 people per square foot of land and sea on this planet. Of course our species would self destruct long before we got to that number!"

"With that many people where would you go on vacation?"

"Because of the one child per family rule in China, for 35 years, its trial in Singapore and the drop in the fertility rate in much of Europe the rate of growth in the world is slowing, but it is not yet reversing. It's still growing at almost 1½% a year. But there are some bright spots.

By 2050 the UN predicts that 25 European nations will have populations below what they are now. Russia will lose 31 million, Italy over 7 million, Poland almost 7 million, and Germany almost 4 million. But the effect is minimized as they take in more refugees. It is predicted that if the current low fertility rate in Japan continues there would be no Japanese left by the middle of the fourth millennium."

"Ya, Japan is really in for some major changes. I did a report on my news program a few months ago. Because of its low birthrate its population has decreased by a couple of million in the last few years. Now in 2025 it's down to 126 million, but 30% of its citizens are over 65. Its median age is 50 years which is 20 years higher than the world average. And in the next thirty years it will lose a quarter of its population. They could bring in foreign workers but the traditional culture of Japan has not been particularly open to people from other cultures and the Japanese written and spoken language is difficult to learn. Unless robotics start doing the work of people, the third strongest economy in the world may drop a few notches. But then Japan leads the world in robotics, so they may not need more workers."

"But if we are to be concerned with the future of the planet, Japan is showing the way. "We should have seen this problem coming. The agricultural surplus allowed more people to leave the farm since fewer were needed to produce the food needed to sustain a technological society, fewer and fewer people were needed to supply all of our physical needs. Factory built housing, advanced construction tools, mass produced autos, clothes and appliances, all reduced the need for hand labor and increased the efficiency of every worker.

"Children became economic drains on their families. Japan and Western Europe are cases in point. In the short term, the next 50 to 100 years, countries' economies will be pinched to deliver pension and health benefits for the increasingly elderly population. Either the fewer workers must pay higher taxes to provide for their elders or the elders must be required to work more years before retiring. General Motors is already in trouble with only one worker for every three retirees."

"Those of us in interesting jobs often don't want to retire. I love my job of researching, interviewing and reporting. But brilliant legislators often force us into an unwanted retirement to make room for the younger workers. So experience is sacrificed for inexperience—hardly a blueprint for efficiency."

"I've enjoyed my life too, Chet. But short sighted people call for more babies to take up the slack. This merely compounds the problem in the long run. Population reduction will obviously have some economic effects. General Motors will sell fewer cars and trucks.

Telephone companies will bill for fewer calls. Airlines will probably fly fewer passengers and oil companies will sell less gasoline. But since the world will have fewer people the standard of living will go up. So there would be economic problems for a few generations while the population stabilizes. It seems to take about 70 years before a population reduction plan is implemented and the society's population actually starts to reduce.

"The longer we continue in this population explosion, the more economically difficult the adjustment will be when we reverse it. But without that major adjustment it will soon be 'sayonara' for our species.

"People who I admire for their ability to think and their concern for the future agree that the world has major problems. Like my old buddy Arnold Toynbee said 'We have been God-like in our planned breeding of our domesticated plants and animals, but we have been rabbit-like in our unplanned breeding of ourselves.' Any growth is bad for the planet but the greatest growth is in the poorer countries. So we have more babies starving to death and fewer children in school. This keeps the poor down and reduces any chance of reducing their poverty. It also fuels their anger and increases civil wars and religious hatreds."

"Wreck, why do you think it fuels religious hate?"

"Well Con, the lack of education limits people's views of options for conflict resolution. If they see the ultimate truth of their lives only in the very limited view of their own tradition; if they understand as truth only what a local religious leader says; if they are not aware that a government based on the laws enacted by the elected representatives of the people may be a better way to go—we will have uneducated prejudices and hatreds. But if they realize that there are highly probable theories in economics and the social sciences that may make them capable of developing economically satisfying lives—then they have a much better chance of seeing the big picture.

"My old professor, Dr. Woellner, said that 'God and one man is a majority.' Certainly truth is not determined by a democratic vote or a Supreme Court decision. De Tocqueville warned us over 150 years ago about the possible tyranny of the majority in America. (4) And 'certainty' is not determined by a single person at the head of a state or a religion. Look at how popes, along with the huge majority of the human race, believed that the earth was flat and that the sun went around the earth. Now the popes, and all educated people, believe just the opposite.

"While Copernicus was admittedly not the first to propose a heliocentric theory of the movement of the sun and Earth, he probably incurred more wrath from his religion than did Nasir al-Din al-Tusi, the thirteenth century Persian Shi'ite when he proposed his theory of planetary motion. Of course at that time Islam was more accepting of science, which is why they were so far ahead of the Christians. And when the Greek Philolaus proposed his heliocentric theory in the fourth century BC he might have drawn a few snickers of disbelief, but the Olympian gods didn't strike him down.

"So how do we approach the religious and state leaders, how do we approach the common people, how do we convince the world's population of the severity of the situation? How do we reduce population while increasing the opportunities for every baby born?

"Certainly if every young person can have the opportunity to learn about the mysteries of science, the flow of history, the enduring questions of ethics—we have a better shot at developing a utopian world where we can live effective and enjoyable lives in a peaceful world."

"You're right Wreck. We don't know how many potential Albert Einsteins, Bill Gateses, Thomas Edisons, Nelson Mandelas, Thomas Jeffersons and Colin Powells are living in huts in Columbia, India, Africa or Bangladesh. The world is really severely handicapping itself when its whole population is not being given the chance to be as well educated as their capabilities will allow. And with globalization and urbanization becoming the rule, working with your hands on a farm or in a factory is less and less likely to be an adequate pursuit for financial success or self fulfillment.

"When I hear of Islamic radicals, like the Taliban, burning down schools in Afghanistan where 70% of the people are illiterate and where millions of children are still not attending school (5), I cringe with pity for the deprived students and for their state that is trying to enter the modern world. I understand the need of some religious leaders to keep people ignorant of their world, and even of their religion so that they can be more easily manipulated. How can an illiterate read the Koran? And you certainly don't want girls in school. The next thing you know they would find out that Muhammad actually liked women and held them in high esteem.

"I have always had the belief that the truly religious people are all climbing the same mountain. They are just climbing from different sides. But those ignorant of the message of the founders of their religions are all fighting at the bottom of the hill. They dig trenches and moats that bring them farther from the top. And their psychotic need to control others and to believe they are right takes them farther from the humility that is needed for sainthood, for union with the Brahman—for Paradise. Just look at the inhumane deeds that have been done in the name of religion—the Crusades, fanatical terrorism, the Inquisition, suicide bombings. The mercy espoused by most great religious teachers is replaced by the most vile human motivation for power and vengeance—a vengeance for either real or imagined wrongs.

"Exactly Con, but we are caught in a Catch 22. The poor people are too uneducated to realize that their procreative profundity is pulling them further and further behind. In Europe we have more people realizing that their own lives will be better without spending their time and money on children. And they have the means of contraception and abortion readily available, so fewer children are being born. If their religious leaders protest, they ignore them.

"On the other hand, the poor are bound up in the tradition of having children and don't have the means to prevent them if they wanted to. They can't see a hope for a better future. But in Europe, Singapore and China—all countries that either have arrived at or are rushing to the gates of plenty, fertility rates are dropping. There is generally a freedom from want in these countries. And there is certainly a good deal of hope, a hope with a good chance of fruition."

"I know that it takes 2.1 children per woman to keep the population stable and I recently read that over 60 countries are now below that level, how high are the rates in the undeveloped parts of the world?"

"They go to almost 6 children per woman in some countries, Lee. Zambia's rate is 5.6. India is 3.1, but that should drop significantly as farming becomes more mechanized and the country becomes more industrialized. Rwanda has a fertility rate of 6 children per woman. The government is now considering recommending only three children per family. The more developed countries average about 1.6 children per woman. The less developed countries average over 3. China, with its one child policy, was still at 1.7 children per woman. And now that the internal pressure forced the rulers to relax the one child policy its rate will go back up. But in Europe, Spain is way down, just 1.15, with Italy not far behind at 1.18. It just goes to show that even in these supposedly Roman Catholic countries, family needs outweigh the commands of religion. By European standards Catholic Ireland has a high fertility rate of 1.9, but that is still a bit below the 2.1 repopulation rate. This naturally increases the percentage of elderly in the population. Europe and Japan are the only regions where the number of people aged 60 and over outnumber the children. Parts of Latin America and Asia are approaching that level. It will necessarily cause an economic hardship for some."

"That 2.1 level is outdated. I know it's used all the time, I heard that same number when I was in college and I understand that it had been around for decades before that. It probably made sense when people died at about 50 but today with the people living into their late 70s and into their 80s it really doesn't apply. Look at this illustration. If we have two people reproducing themselves at 20 we now have four people. If those children reproduce by the time they are 20 we now have six people alive. If those children reproduced by the time they are 20 than by age 80 we would have 8 people, not the original two. If we assume that the original parents die at about 80 you'd actually have six of their descendants still living. If this were true today instead of having 8 billion people we would have three or four times that many.

"But reproducing yourself at the age of 20, while it might be common in the underdeveloped countries it is not common in the more developed nations. So let's assume that the people reproduce themselves by the time they are 35. So now there are four people, the two parents and two children. Then let's assume that those children reproduce themselves by the time they are 35. We now have six living people and the original parents are now 70 years old. So you can see that with today's increasing lifespans that 2.1 fertility idea doesn't work—certainly not for the near term.. But with far longer lifespans it is probably more like one child per couple to maintain the population. But maintaining our 8 billion people is not our objective. We need to reduce the population not maintain it.

"As a conservative I am concerned with the strong religious beliefs among those few religions that espouse high fertility. They can skew the numbers upward. For example while the fertility rates m Europe are coming down dramatically, Muslims who have come to Europe as workers or refugees are expected to have fertility rates of 3.4. (6) Population projections are that in the century from 1950 to 2050 the world Muslim population percentage will have doubled, from 14 to 27%, and their actual population will have increased from 360 million to 2.5 billion. Catholics will be about half that number and Protestants will equal Catholics. So Christians and Muslims will be about equal, but the Muslims are gaining at a faster rate. Non-Hispanic whites, who were the majority of Christians earlier, will be only about 20% of the 3 billion Christians because the increases will be primarily in Africa, South America, and Asia—the areas of lower education levels and greater poverty.

"Hindus have lost some ground, especially to the Muslims. This worries somePoliticians in Kolbata, concerned that Hindus are losing population, condemned birth control and proposed instituting rewards for women who had at least 10 children. (7)

"This illustrates a basic view of some religious leaders that their religion must be the largest and take over the world. It also is a tactic of some national leaders who take the short sighted view that more people are needed in their country to pay for their social welfare programs, to make up their armies or to provide consumers for their businesses that want to expand."

"As the years flow by we find that the more educated people are finding problems either in believing in a creator, or in religions' paths to salvation. Morality is no longer necessarily a religious domain as it had become under the Mideastern monotheistic religions of Judaism, Christianity and Islam. The social democratic concept of respect for the person has become more pervading. This may or may not be associated with a religious context but can be merely based on a secular idea.

"Since religions tend to enrich themselves, rather than their followers, many wonder if it is not more difficult for the religious leaders to enter the Kingdom of Heaven than for a camel to pass through the eye of a needle as Matthew wrote in Chapter 19, verse 24.

Mosques, temples and churches hold so much gold while the faithful adherents to the religion are starving in the back pews and outside the holy walls. How much food and medicine would the golden domes, the art collections, the real estate holdings and the gilded idols bring if they were sold on the open market?

"Europe has become far more secular over the years. The U.S. has a 95% population of believers, and many are churchgoers, but the American Catholics are nearly identical in their daily lives to the Protestants. They use contraceptives just as often. They have just as many abortions. They don't follow the same political party lines in elections. They act as if they are secular—except for a few hours on Sunday. So unless the more secular states want their grandchildren to be ruled by Christian or Islamic regimes, such as in the Middle Ages, they must give some thought to preserving the progress made from the Period of Enlightenment and the rise of secular democracies.

"The lack of education and the unwillingness to study and understand divergent views is a major problem with fundamentalists. You remember back in 2006 when an Afghan, who had renounced Islam for Christianity fifteen years earlier, was brought to court because the new Afghan Constitution required that nothing could go against the Koran. And the Koran prescribes death for one who renounces Islam. By contrast in the West, Islam is accepted as a legitimate religion. Religious beliefs, but not all religious practices, are tolerated.

"Of course with European educations, the Muslims may follow the patterns of the Christians by reducing their family size, particularly if state welfare payments are insufficient to support them. Unlimited social welfare for all is an idea that is, by necessity, evolving into a limited social welfare for the needy. The European post-World War II social welfare states, that came into being when the populations were young, are being re-evaluated and diminished as the populations age. This also forces a re-direction of their once vibrant economies. Even oil-rich Norway, a social welfare model, is not handling all of its cradle to grave promises.

"Now in many countries financial pressure is often being exerted on parents, both married and unmarried, who cannot support their broods. These are nearly always people with low levels of education.

"It seems that fundamentalists in all religions are seldom well educated. They may know their holy books and have an interpretation of certain passages, often at odds with the interpretations of others in their religion, but they don't have a broad knowledge of history or science or a comprehensive understanding of philosophy or theology. Their thinking seems to be simply that their Supreme Being exists, He gave them their holy scripture, and He agrees 100% with them no matter what their interpretations of His scriptures are.

"With them all thinking somewhat differently, whether in the same religion or different religions, you'd think that some might wonder about God's omniscience, letting so many thousands of holy people each think they have the inspired word, when their views are so different. This is a bit different from Las Vegas where a gambler "knows" he has a "sure thing" but still recognizes there is a chance that he won't win.

"Maybe we should send all these holy men to the 'Sin City' with a hundred dollars and tell them just to bet on the sure things when God tips them. Just think of all the gold they can win to gild their churches and mosques! And if God doesn't give them all the right cards, maybe it will make them realize that perhaps they have occasionally misinterpreted the Almighty's message. What do you want to say Ray?"

"As your resident reactionary, and I don't like that epithet! I have to point out some problems with reducing the population. There is the Biblical command to "Be fruitful and multiply." There is also the sin of Onan cited in Genesis 38 verses 9 and 10 in which "he spilled his seed on the ground" to avoid procreating—and God slew him. Whether his sin was masturbation or coitus interruptus or just not fulfilling the law of marrying his brother's wife—Onan committed a pretty dastardly sin. As a Catholic I follow the teachings of St. Augustine and the popes in believing that his sin was related to contraception. Because, as you know, contraception while actively participating in sexual intercourse is a sin. Consequently the only method available to Catholics is abstinence. This therefore allows only the so called 'rhythm method' for Catholic married couples.

"But there are social concerns also. How are you going to pay the pensions of the graying populations with fewer younger workers? The realities of pension funding, for example, is a huge dent in the national budget. In Italy 12% of the country's gross national product goes to pensions—and it will be going higher. You must have young workers to pay for the pensions of the old.

"I have heard that the earth can handle 16 billion people. If so, we are a long way from hitting that mark. So when you talk about the religious leaders who advocate more children don't you think that they are also thinking?

"And the Pope is certainly concerned about the plight of children. I think it was in about 2008 at his Christmas Mass that he sent out an appeal to help those children who are forced to live in the streets, those who are forced into armies and those who are otherwise abused. He asked the faithful to help those children who are denied parental love and the millions who are exploited in so many ways. He was emphatic that we must help those suffering children. Looks like you disagree Wreck."

"No offense Ray, but while Pope Benedict was recognizing the problem, he didn't suggest any solutions and his vehement stands against contraception and abortion are the major impediments to alleviating the suffering. It is easy to recognize many of the problems that plague our planet, but suggesting workable solutions, then implementing them, are the requirements for progress in problem solving. I believe many religious leaders think that they are thinking freely, but they are so bound up by their basic assumptions from the literature of the past that they cannot be concerned with the future of our world as science is predicting it. We will, no doubt, have this discussion again. Let's pick it up after we have our discussions with Dr. Wang in Kino.

"But certainly not all religions oppose population control. For example, the General Assembly of the Presbyterian Church reaffirmed their existing policies on population and, in view of the compelling need now for fewer births, they called for 'encouragement and support, respect and honor' to be accorded to couples who choose not to conceive children as well as to those who choose to conceive. Other religious groups have called for the same concern for overpopulation."

"It's clear that, just as so many individual and national decisions are made for economic reasons, limiting family size is largely an economic decision. And I've certainly seen it out in the business world. So many women are excited about their careers in business, medicine, law and sales that staying home with children is generally not that appealing."

"I guess that's true Con. I've been away from the business world so long that I'm not really in tune. But I see my daughter who is totally devoted to her two children. She's very successful in pharmaceutical sales, which she loves—but then can't wait to get home to her husband and kids. She loves her job and loves her family. She feels doubly blessed."

"Oh, I know a number of women who are in that category. But they can't do everything that they would like. There's little time for housecleaning, so they hire a cleaning service. They don't have as much time for R & R with their husbands. They can't leave the kids every weekend for skiing, surfing, general vacationing—but those are not their priorities. We have to realize that we are not all cut out of the same cloth."

"We are going to get a chance to discuss these psychological differences when we get to Singaling. Dr. Chan is one of the foremost experts in the world in this area. After we pick Dr. Wang's brain about value systems and how we each vary in our values then learn about our needs and drives from Dr. Chan we should have a clearer insight into why we do what we do, and perhaps how we can fashion more satisfying lives for ourselves by understanding us better. I believe that our beliefs and actions are based either on our unconscious motivations or on our values. And commonly we act psychologically but believe that our actions are really value based—which they are not. "

"Wreck, I'm really excited about discussing life with these people. Who else do you have lined up to help us open our minds?"

"There are a bunch of things I would like to delve more deeply into. How do you get things to happen is one concern. If we were to seriously pursue licensing parents what methods would be available? Con?"

"We would be looking at politics there! Politics is the 'science of the possible' is what my old UCLA professor taught me. Dr. Titus was THE expert on how people can and should be treated, depending on the desired ends. Remember him Wreck? Juniors sat in the last rows, seniors ahead of them, then the masters students then the PhD students in the front. Titus said that since it was a class in "the science of the possible" any way that you could get a grade was OK. I remember you knew one teaching assistant from when she was a high school student coming to your lifeguard tower, then you started dating the other TA. And you got an A."

"I remember it well. Probably the only smart thing I did in college! But Con, I think we will find that what works politically, that is how we get people to do things, goes back to the original motivational ideas of values, needs and drives. But the effective politicians are able to show us why we should follow their leadership--often without thinking."

"This sounds enlightening. Anything else planned?"

"Of course, we're going to solve all the world's problems! We are going to Muchinju, that experimental religious country where people of the several major religions are getting along quite well. I want to see how peace and population control have worked in our modern world.

"But then there are the United Colonies where I think that freedom has gotten out of control. They are making some highly controversial changes in their system to try to curb the urban excesses that seem to accompany the materially induced selfishness of our modern global economic and social monster. They have had to try to reconcile the ideals of liberty and equality---which are actually antithetical. They chose liberty. They have a total aversion to both population control and to licensing parents. But they do make parents totally responsible for their children!

"Another stop I plan would be in Northland. Their approach to population control and to parent licensing is really far out. They are doing human cloning and artificial insemination to 'improve the human breed' so to speak."

"You mean eugenics?"

"Yes. Eugenics in ways that Hitler or Churchill never dreamed of!"

"Well Wreck, I don't know which adventures look forward to more—traveling the physical or the intellectual world.

"Wreck, as the resident liberal of the group, I share your concerns about population control. The genocide in Africa is appalling. Estimates are that nearly 4 million people were killed in Congo in the war of 1998. A half million Tutsis and moderate Hutus were slaughtered by rampaging Hutus in a hundred days. Millions more have become internally displaced or have sought asylum in neighboring countries. My cousin is in an African aid group. She says nobody outside of the country seems to care. She's told me about seeing five year olds with their hands cut off by the invading army. Ten year old girls raped and tortured. Villages burned down.

"Sub-Saharan Africa has one crisis after another. Then we have the Philippines, Palestine, Iraq, Syria and North Africa--country after country engaged in generally meaningless attempts to kill off their neighbors. Columbia has a perpetual civil war. U.N. High Commissioner for Refugees António Guterres recently reported that there are more people displaced now than at any time since World War II.

"Obviously the planet is not the home of universal happiness. And for the good life we certainly passed the maximum population some time ago, if two billion people is the maximum load the earth can endure. Fewer would obviously be better. By 2050 the population may stabilize at 10 billion people. With ¼ child less per woman we would reach 2 billion in 2300. But can we survive 200 more years with the scarcities of water and power and with polluted air and water? We need to do it faster."

"Nature will handle the situation if we don't. And nature can be more brutal than we are. Diseases will take their toll. Untreatable tuberculosis kills a few million a year. When I left the planet there were 40 million with AIDS and over 20 million had died from it. Was this a blessing or a curse? The life expectancy in Zimbabwe had fallen from 60 to 30. But they can still produce a number of children before they are 30 and most of the children will be HIV positive.

"Nature seems to be trying to limit populations Along with HIV we have ebola, malaria, famines, influenzas, tidal waves, wars, uprisings, volcanic eruptions, hurricanes and earthquakes. And if those don't control the total world population then we have homosexual partnerships, assuming they don't have children. The power drive of political madmen from Genghis Khan, Alexander and Caesar to Hitler, Pol Pot and Hussein have worked to kill off both soldiers and civilians. Weapons of mass destruction, now available to most power hungry leaders and fanatics, can control populations more effectively and sadistically today than at any time in the past. Poison the water supply of a city, let loose deadly pathogens in the air, use nuclear weapons against major cities like New York, London, Tokyo, Beijing or Paris.

"Or maybe we'll follow the pattern of Dr. Calhoun's mice. Maybe it will be done through a worldwide atomic war. But wouldn't it be 'loverly' if we would solve it with our intelligence? And restricting births is the most obvious solution. But further, allowing children to be born to the best possible parents certainly is an altruistic goal.

"Would it be better to reduce the population voluntarily, with its rather minor adjustment problems or should we wait for the devastation that Mother Nature and her psychotic warrior sons will undoubtedly wreak? Which approach will result in the least amount of human suffering?"

"Tell me about it, Wreck! Human history is little more than recanting the wars of conquerors and religious liberators advancing their causes while eliminating the heretics. As a utopian, I can't help but hope that we can end wars, increase education and toleration, and save our planet. But the realities of human nature, as shown from our history, tell me that it is improbable. Still I hope for the best. I hope that reason will overcome our selfishness—and that our logical potentials will win out over our psychological propensities."

"Well Lee, I would like to think that we could live in a stress free utopian world, but the classical utopian ideals can't be reached today. At least I don't think so. Every utopia requires that people give up some freedoms and desires. It may be the family, private property, some controls on freedom of speech or of the press. The task is to keep as many freedoms as possible while controlling population increases through education, rewards and punishments. The rewards might be financial, educational, vocational or recreational. The punishments might also be financial, educational and vocational and might also include imprisonment.

"H.G. Wells in Modern Utopia rightly said that the utopian plans of the past postulated a content citizenry, but no society can exist without friction, conflicts and wastes. In my search for utopia, I am really just looking for a better way for today and the dawn of tomorrow. Obviously if Plato or More were writing today they would have quite different plans for their societies. Economics change. Political realities change. No one would plan a utopia based on a small state like Plato did with Sparta. Today a globalized utopia would be the goal. But the prejudices of the people, the roles of religions and the call of a democratic freedom push and pull the possibilities for order. The best we can hope for is that we can agree on stopping the population explosion, reducing the violence, stopping the global warming, and installing workable democracies that allow for freedom and universal education. We can't eliminate poverty until these are accomplished. We can't eliminate diseases until we can control our environment. We can't eliminate our self imposed inhumanity to our human neighbors until we make the pragmatic changes that need to be made. But just what changes can be made and should be prioritized? That's what I want to concentrate on.

"There are a number of ways society might work to reduce childbirth, especially to young mothers. One might make it illegal to have a child before 18. Twenty-five would even be better. I understand that if pregnancies were prevented until 25 it could reduce the number of children born worldwide by about 40%. But while such methods might easily reduce population they might not increase the happiness of those children.

"I don't like America's approach to limiting population. Our Constitutional freedom to own guns helps by having psychos shooting school children, that way they'll never reproduce. Then, of course, our gangs kill each other repeatedly. That reduces our population and saves money on prisons—the dead guys won't commit any more crimes. Then there are the accidental shootings of children by parents and parents by children, But then—that's the American way!

LICENSING PARENTS

"So let me talk about my other concern, licensing parents. In the early 1900s maybe a few people dreamed of space travel. But did any even conceive of television, computers, the internet, artificial hearts, atomic power? There were probably no such dreams, and certainly no concrete plans to achieve any dreams that might have existed. But to reduce population is not just a dream but a very real need—probably the greatest need that we humans have ever encountered. And there is a plan. It is already being done in some countries. And that plan is aimed at fulfilling the hope that every child born into the diminishing population is loved and cared for, is educated, and is given every opportunity to live a satisfying and socially worthwhile life. Effective parenting licensing is the answer to both problems."

"Wreck, would you still advocate licenses if the birthrate were being reduced in most countries?"

"Yes Ray. We still need to protect children until all are guaranteed an effective childhood, where every child is loved, cared for and effectively educated. If you know any teachers or social workers you can find out about the number of parents in every walk of life, that abuse their children. Children should be wanted and parents should be taught what their children need in order to grow up effectively. They need to know about their physical, emotional and mental needs. And potential parents should be screened to make certain that their own emotional maturity levels are mature enough to be able to raise a child. I think it's a shame that a half million children in the U.S. are being raised in foster homes. Research shows that more children are being raised by grandparents than parents. Then look at the number being   raised by TV and video games. Seems to me that there aren't as many children who are really wanted as most people would like to believe. 'Making the baby' is obviously more fun than 'making the child' for the great majority. And a child has only one childhood. It must be the best and most loving experience possible

"When the state of South Dakota passed its anti-abortion law, excepting only to save the life of the mother, even rape victims could not have an abortion. And South Dakota has an extremely high rape level. I assume that the legislators know that every child of a rape will have a mother who is as financially and emotionally secure and loving as the average child born to a happily married couple. We can certainly assume that any raped mother will desperately want the child that was conceived in violence, fear, desperation and hate. And if the rapist doesn't marry her he will certainly send his monthly support checks.

"You probably read the best selling book Freakonomics (8) it theorized that the major reason that crime has dropped is that the Supreme Court allowed abortion in Roe v. Wade twenty years earlier. Poorer women, whose children would most likely find their way into gangs and crime, procured abortions and thus reduced the number of potential criminals.

"Is it really more important to just have a baby born or is it more important to have a baby born who will be wanted and loved and will have the opportunity for a healthy and satisfying life? Wouldn't you support abortion in that case Ray?"

"Never! The Church's position is that the soul is infused into the fertilized ovum at the instant of conception. That should be perfectly clear to any thinking person. Aren't you a thinking person, Wreck?"

"Well I don't know enough to argue about that issue right now, but I know it's something I will ask Dr. Wang about when we get to Kino."

"Even without the religious concerns, in the more primitive societies children are often economic assets. They are the necessary hands for tilling the fields and they are the essential old age security for their parents."

"That's true Ray, so if we reduce a population something would have to be done to set up government care for the elderly who don't have children. But you would have to agree that in the non-agricultural, developed economies-- children cost money. Some families are happier with children, most are not. Children are no longer economically useful because there are fewer small farms and the labor is machine-generated, not human-generated.

"I've thought about this most of the time I was in space. Our biggest problem right now is how to convince the people, the politicians and all the religious leaders that population must be controlled. Is it the will of Allah to see the human race in misery? Is it the will of God to see His world heading for oblivion. Did the Supreme Being give humans intelligence to control their instincts and change their traditions?

"I think that voluntary population control with the increased possibility of loving parents will make the world safer for all. And it should reduce the number of warrior leaders and terrorists in the world because more children will be shown the path to loving rather than loathing, helping rather than hating. I know that in Norway one in three new mothers is over 30. I would guess that they would be more financially secure and psychologically mature than your average 17 year old mother in LA.

"Think about it. Look at the laws for licensing we have enacted. What is more important for society, dogs on a leash or concerned and loving parents, driving a car or increasing the chances that humankind can live peacefully and in a friendly environment without famine and pollutions? If it's more important should it be licensed to ensure that the most important things are a legitimate concern of the society?"

"But Wreck, licensing parents would be genocide because the poor and uneducated would most likely not be given licenses. Poor Indians and sub-Saharan blacks would obviously be targeted."

Chet had sat quietly but felt compelled to enter the free-for-all.

"Ray wouldn't you call what the Africans are doing to each other genocide? When I covered Africa for World News I was appalled by the cruelty and killing. They didn't seem to see it as genocide, at least not as racial genocide. It's not a racial thing to license parents. It is a human thing. But a proposal for licensing would certainly run into incredible opposition and in America and most other countries would be politically impossible to accomplish. The Christians, particularly the Catholics and Mormons, the Muslims, and the national rulers who don't want their constituencies reduced, business people who want to expand the consumer base, and certainly the tradition of having children—will be huge obstacles."

"What if we make it voluntary Chet,—money or free education for voluntary sterilization or having small families—money direct to the people—bypassing the leaders. Today billions are given to eradicate disease in Africa. Even if diseases are controlled, the poor will be even poorer and more miserable if they continue to produce large numbers of children. There have to be financial incentives for today and for the future to motivate them effectively.

"Don't you think that we have a duty to make every child's life worthwhile. With death by hunger, genocide and disease rampant in Third World countries and with mental illness, abuse and the lack of optimal opportunities throughout the world in all societies, protection of children is an essential. If they are to be born, society owes them the best chance at a healthy, happy and useful life."

"Don't you all agree that children should be properly parented? But most people want the right to have children—as many as they want. They may call it a human right. But others call for children's human rights to have the best parents possible. Sometimes these proposed human rights, those of the potential parents and those of the children, are in conflict.

"Do you think that the 13 year old father and the 15 year old mother who had a child in the UK in 2008 can properly parent their child? Alfie Patton, who sired the child when he was 12 and whose voice had not yet changed, told a reporter that 'I thought it would be good to have a baby. I didn't think about how we would afford it. I don't really get pocket money. My dad sometimes gives me £10. . . . We wanted to have the baby but were worried about how people would react. I didn't know what it would be like to be a dad. I will be good, though, and care for it.'(8a)

"What about that unmarried unemployed Los Angeles woman who had octuplets after already mothering six children under the age of eight. And with three of those children were handicapped! And all living with her mother in a three bedroom house! Seems to me that these children won't have an optimal start in life—even in California.

"To protect children we have laws requiring car seats and laws to require that parents not lock them in cars when they go shopping. We require that they go to school or have adequate home schooling. Schools may require vaccinations to protect the child from a disease. Government has introduced child labor laws, standards for required financial child support, and now often holds the parents responsible for the crimes of their children.

"Government increasingly has moved to protect children from the possible abuse by parents or others. No thinking informed person would say that there are not some parents in the world who are incompetent or abusive.

"I remember a story in the Los Angeles Times many years ago in which it was reported that criminally abusive parents, after being released from prison, were given their young children back. Within three days the three year old girl was dead from exhaustion because her father forced her to continue running around the house while periodically beating her. I cried, and still do when remembering the story. My daughter was three at the time. To think of her being similarly abused sickened me beyond belief.

"A friend told me about witnessing the boyfriend of a neighbor standing a little girl on a table then punching her hard enough to knock her to the floor, then standing her up and repeating the process. My neighbor called the police who took the hateful Satan to jail. But that didn't remove the physical or psychological scars from the little girl. These abuses are not confined just to little girls, although girls seem to be the major objects of abuse. When professional football player Laveranues Coles told his team, then the world, that he had been sexually abused by his stepfather for years, at gunpoint, it shocked the nation.

"How many abusing or murdering parents should society tolerate? 1%, 10%? How many children should be allowed to be sexually abused by parents or others? How many should be allowed to be psychologically abused? How many should we allow to be born with AIDS? How many should be allowed to be born into abject poverty? How many should suffer through childhood continually malnourished? The ideal would be none! We probably can't get to that level, but we can certainly reduce the number."

Lee couldn't restrain himself any longer.

"I was talking to an industrial psychologist at my office the other day. He said that how a child is going to be treated may already be predetermined before the baby is conceived. If a mother wants to have the family she never had in her lifetime, then the child is going to have to make her feel that she has a warm, loving family. Later, when the child wants to do things on his own the mother may see it as a threat to her preconceived need for a close family. She is using the child to fulfill her needs, rather than being an effective parent and helping the child to satisfy its own needs and developing its potentials.

"Young pregnant unmarried girls I have talked to almost universally want a baby so they will have someone to love them. Obviously this is the reverse of what is needed for a baby. Babies need someone who can love them and help them to grow mentally and emotionally. In fact it takes maturity to be able to love, and no child has such maturity. It is the job of the parent to develop the self-respect in the child that is fundamental to being able to love. Another reason young girls may want children is because it proves that they are adults. So adulthood is thought of as strictly biological, not involving mental or emotional maturity, not involving any ability to financially take care of oneself, not involving any socially useful purpose.

"I've heard young men say that the reason they wanted a child is to carry on the family name. This is another disservice to the child. Children should be conceived so that they can become physically and emotionally healthy people, not so that their parents can indulge some adolescent need or feeling. This just continues the train of insecure needy people who don't have the emotional requirements for raising an emotionally healthy child. And what about babies born to crack addicted mothers, mothers with AIDS, alcoholic mothers who risk inflicting their babies with fetal alcohol syndrome?

"Do you remember that back in January of 2016 David Cameron, the Prime Minister of the UK, suggested that all parents take classes on how to raise their children. This is obviously too late, but it is still a step in the right direction. Naturally there were those resisting the proposal calling it a 'nanny' state move. But no one could disagree with the fact that there were far too many children who were rebellious, lazy, drank too much, did not study, entered lives of crime, became early and ineffective parents and were anchors to the economic and social progress of the society."

"Lee, I should probably do a TV show on this subject. If children have any rights how can they be protected? Actually they don't have any rights if society doesn't spell them out and enforce them. Many elements in society are doing a great deal to protect what they call the rights of the unborn. Some even murder living adults, particularly doctors who perform abortions, but there is no such zeal to protect a child once it is born. Is that logical? Shouldn't all children have the right to develop their potentials fully?"

"That would be a good idea, Chet. I know a couple of attorneys in my firm who would help you put it together. But Wreck, I see several potential problems when suggesting that parents be licensed. One is that when you suggest something that flies in the face of a tradition, especially a tradition that began as a cultural imperative—you are going to have problems. But back to your licensing proposal, you must admit that there are a few stumbling blocks to licensing parents to have children."

"More than a few! Some would say that to have children is a command by God to 'be fruitful and multiply.' We find it in both Genesis 1 and 9. Some would say that it is a right, like the rights to freedom of speech and religion, even though it is not spelled out in the Constitution. However legal limits have been placed on freedom of speech. And freedom of religion limits human sacrifice and usually does not allow handling poisonous snakes or drinking poison. (9) Even refusing medical treatment on religious grounds is not always allowed. Legal decisions exist that both allow and disallow the state to preempt the refusal of medical treatment for children because of religious beliefs."

"You're talking law now, so let me add my two cents worth. Many modern societies grant the right of free speech, but it is not without limits. In fact in the United States the right to say just about anything seems to be possible. While the oft quoted remark of Supreme Court Justice Oliver Wendell Holmes (10) that 'you don't have the right to yell 'fire' in a crowded theater' may have once been the standard of the law, the right to free speech has been significantly loosened. For example the Supreme Court of the U.S. found it to be a legal use of free speech when it allowed a Ku Klux Klan member to advocate the killing of Jews and 'niggers.'(11)

"The free speech of Socrates was muted in ancient Athens, when his gadfly bite forced those who were able—to think. So he drank the hemlock and society was again at peace—the peace that comes with the certainty of tradition and the bliss of ignorance.

"Following the subway bombings in London, Muslim cleric Hamza al-Masri was sentenced to seven years in prison for inciting the killing of non-believers—particularly through joining al-Qaeda. His rhetoric was certainly fiery. But at about the same time there were no arrests made of Muslims demonstrating against the notorious Danish cartoons, even though the demonstrators called for the extermination of those who mocked Islam. And in England, two far right wing agitators, who were arrested for attempting to rile up the crowd to attack the wicked religion of Islam, were acquitted in court.

"Freedom of religion is also not absolute. It must always be seen in terms of compelling state interests. (12) The U.S. has found that a military uniform can not include a religious article of clothing such as a yarmulke (13) On the other hand when a religious group used, for religious purposes, a tea that contained an hallucinogenic drug that is otherwise banned in the U.S. and throughout most of the world, the U.S. Supreme Court unanimously ruled that the government had not proven that banning the drug in this case had demonstrated a compelling state interest. (14) Another way to refute a religious liberty is to prove that 'a clear and present danger' to the state exists. Such a danger is often hard to prove."

"So you're saying that to allow parent licensing in the U.S. judges would have to be convinced that it was a 'compelling state interest' or that not licensing would present a 'clear and present danger' to the state of the nation? Or maybe that certain potential parents would probably provide a 'clear and present danger' to their planned child."

"Those are possibilities. 'Difficult cases make bad law' is an old law school saying. When a severe case, such as one that threatens society, is dealt with severely, how can the society deal less harshly with a similar case that tends to back up the present prejudices of the society?

"We don't allow unlimited freedom. People who may be a danger to themselves or others may be removed from society and placed in mental institutions or prisons. In other cases we require licensing or a specified level of education before allowing certain activities, such as doctoring or filling prescriptions. Look at how many types of activities have been licensed— car drivers, truck drivers, teachers, child care centers, dentists, contractors, real estate sales people, psychologists, the list goes on and on. And which of these activities is more important than parenting?

"We are so often prisoners of our times. A woman who wanted an abortion in 1850 was imprisoned more often then than she would be today. Today if she lives in an area where it is illegal, there is often a nearby area where it is permitted so a few hours by plane or train and she is in a different, more permissive, time and place."

"As in many important cases we have one person's perceived rights versus another person's perceived rights. Few 'rights' are universal—maybe none are. "Don't murder someone in your own society" is a generally recognized 'right' and duty, but it is certainly not universally adhered to. Street gangs regularly murder others. Secret state organizations like the CIA of the USA, FSB as the successor of the KGB in Russia, or the Israeli Mossad regularly kill others in their societies. Genocides in Africa have people in the same state and same tribe killing each other.

"And what society are we talking about? The world society as seen by the United Nations? Our nation? Then what about civil wars? If I am a gang member is my society only my street gang?

"Treason is a universal no-no whether it is to the general society or to the gang. But sometimes the traitors become heroes—patriots. Look at the instigators of the American and French Revolutions.

"Talking about rights, in today's world few people have the legal right to terminate their own lives, even if they are suffering horribly. Only a few countries grant this right to euthanasia. You may not even have the right to refuse medical treatment. So these highly personal desires are seldom 'rights' in the societies in which we live.

"Also, your rights may shift depending on who is in authority. The right to an abortion may be rescinded by a new legislature or a new court. Your Constitutional 'right' to practice your religion as you see fit can be affirmed by one court even if you are breaking serious laws, such as using potentially dangerous psychoactive drugs or are handling poisonous snakes and drinking strychnine. An absolute monarch, of course, has the power to control your actions, but even a democratic government, based on laws can take away what one thinks is a 'right.' And often what one thinks is a 'right' is nothing more than a selfish desire. It does not have the legal governmental sanctions to make it a 'right.'

"Some parents have been sterilized to prevent them from having children. There was a eugenics movement in the United States and northern Europe during the first half of the 20th Century. It allowed sterilization of some potential parents, usually due to mental incompetence. These laws have generally been rescinded, but a U.S. Supreme court case (15) allowed a state institutionalized imbecile, who was both the child and the mother of other imbeciles, to be sterilized. However in a later case a man who was merely a criminal was not required to have a state sterilization because he had not been granted due process. But the way was still clear for sterilizations in other instances. (16)

"Legally the state is in loco parentis, 'in place of the parents'. And while the state does not want to get into the business of raising children, it often must take over where the parents have proven unable or incompetent."

"Gosh Lee, I didn't realize that we had such court decisions. You lawyers and judges have sure screwed up our country!"

"Point taken, but now Wreck, what requirements would you propose for a license if it were legal?"

"I have some ideas but I want to visit some of the countries that have enacted licensing and see what they propose and how their programs are proceeding. It does bother me that some religions advocate large families but expect that their own or other societies will pay for them. I wonder how this is being handled in countries that require licenses."

"Who are you suggesting should determine the qualifications for parenthood Wreck?"

"Psychologists, family counselors, teachers, even the electorate could be involved. But one reason we're going to take this trip is to observe what some nations have done. So let's hold off on this one for a while. And remember the idea is not necessarily to only license potential ideal parents but rather to eliminate those who have little or no competence at the time they apply for the license. Those who are likely to mistreat their children would be eliminated. We would certainly want to make certain that there was financial ability. We would want to assess the emotional maturity to be unselfish relative to the child's needs."

"Psychologists? I hear that generally people study psychology to throw suspicion off themselves! But let's say you come up with a decent test. How would you know that your elite parent candidates won't someday abuse their children. How are you going to weed out the sexual predators? We certainly had that problem among some priests and look at the screening and education we have all had to go through."

"At this stage of our knowledge of emotional development we can't be absolutely certain. Just like we are not certain that a doctor who passes the medical boards will be able to diagnose without error or to operate perfectly every time. Science is about probabilities not certainties. If even the lowest 1% of the worst possible parents were eliminated we would have accomplished something positive for the children of our nation and our world. But there have been tests developed which have been proven to be quite accurate, although not infallible.

"But on with our discussion. I suppose that getting a license would be no real problem to responsible people, but might create great anger and frustration among those who were denied a license."

Ray was furious, or at least as angry as a man of God might be."

"There is certainly the possibility of prejudicial factors affecting licensing. What if the licensing board didn't like us Catholics. What if the examiners were anti-black or anti-white or anti-poor or anti-Semitic? If Hitler's Germany were licensing do you think any Jews or gypsies would have been given licenses? If bin Laden were the examiner would Christian Germans get licenses? But Hitler might have given a license to any blond beast, no matter how abusive he might become and bin Laden would happily have given licenses to any potential terrorist. So I think there are more objections to licensing parents than just going against the Scriptures."

"I'm not sure that the Scriptures would prevent reducing population or making certain that parents were fit to have children. In fact a number of Protestant denominations have come out for population reduction. Some Muslim groups too. But go on, Ray."

"There's nothing more personal than having a family. I'd say it is more of a basic right than is freedom of speech. People who want children are going to do their best for them. It just amazes me that you, my old buddy, have taken the same kind of path that Hitler might have taken—and in fact did in some cases."

"Wait a minute padre. I know you've studied more philosophy than I have, but you know that bringing in Hitler is a logical fallacy. You have to stick to arguing the issues, not bringing in some extraneous issue. You know that logical fallacies have been postulated and explained since the time of Aristotle. And saying that an idea is bad because a bad person also holds that idea is one of the logical fallacies we must avoid.

"Hitler did some good things and some bad things according to historians. Pope John Paul did some good things and some bad things according to some. So stick to the issues.

What if Hitler ate fish and apples. Those are both good nutritional habits. Would you stop eating apples because Hitler ate them? You know as well as I do that logical fallacies have been used to convince people to follow certain courses of action even though any truly rational thinker can see through the holes in the logic."

"Well Wreck, you're right about that. I'm going to have to watch my inductive and deductive reasoning and not let them get in the way of my passion. So what if a person didn't pass the licensing test?"

"I would assume that in most cases any deficiencies could be made up. If it were that they were too young, they would grow up. If it were financial they could earn more money. If it were a lack of knowledge, they could take courses to make it up. If it were demonstrated abusive behavior, there might be anger management therapy. If it were drug abuse, they could get treatment. I would think that most deficiencies could be made up by people honestly desiring to be parents.

"In democratic countries we would assume that an enlightened approach to parenting would be possible. Certainly there would be appeals to higher levels of the licensing departments and eventually to the courts."

"How would you enforce such procedures? What if a couple had an unlicensed child?"

"We're going to look at how others have handled the problem in our travels. Maybe we don't need to reinvent the wheel. Or maybe we'll get our own ideas on how to handle it. I'm sure glad you're going Ray. You'll certainly keep me on my toes.

"Guys, let's try to keep our eyes on the big picture. Whose rights are to be protected? The rights of parents, whether competent or incompetent? The rights of a child—the certainty of love, of feeling safe and of belonging. The needs of a society? The needs of the human race? The desires of a religion to have more members? Remember that studies show that in our country half of all children born are unwanted. (16a) What are the chances that an unwanted child will be treated as well as a child who was desired? It seems that social and legal thinking is moving more toward the rights of the child and the rights of the state and away from what many adults think are their parental 'rights.' In fact parental duties to the child, for the sake of the child and that of the state, is becoming more important."

"As a priest I still think that it is a totalitarian idea and it seems to smack of a eugenics approach to having children. You may not like it when I bring up Hitler, but those were two major factors in his Nazi philosophy."

"We've already discussed eugenics. Yes it was tried in Nazi Germany but it was also attempted in the United States and in other non-totalitarian states. And it is still allowed in certain cases.

"I don't know if this is an argument for eugenics, but in Israel there were recently over 600 cases of handicapped children suing parents and doctors for "wrongful birth" because of the unhappy lives they have been forced to live since their birth. At this time there are meetings being held to determine whether such suits are legitimate. (16b) There are numerous questions that must be addressed, such as: how many tests should be given to a pregnant woman to ascertain probabilities of giving birth to a handicapped child and whether or not doctors must prescribe such tests to protect them from malpractice suits. There is also the question of how much additional money that society must spend on handicapped children.

"But let's look at your concern with totalitarianism. Totalitarianism, as the word suggests, is the full control of the totality, or of the major facets, of the lives of those subject to it. What Lee?"

"'Totalitarian' is a negatively charged word. It means that the governing body exerts absolute or nearly absolute control, on the members of the subordinated group. Strong rulers are often either completely or partially totalitarian. Stalin's USSR was such a government. It was totalitarian in its control of the economy and in its state atheism. But it allowed people to pursue educations, for which they were qualified, and it provided recreational opportunities without much interference. The Catholic Church is totalitarian. Just look at its requirements for only male priests, for an unmarried clergy, for its opposition to mechanical, hormonal and chemical contraception and to abortion. When the Pope speaks ex cathedra he gives his commands to all of his followers. As with the Soviet regime, he allows free education and recreation—as long as that recreation doesn't include pre-marital sex. Hitler had a totalitarian control. Generals nearly always exert such control—the orders come down from the top and the underlings must execute them or be guilty of insubordination, which might result in imprisonment or execution.

"Certainly a totalitarian regime is more efficient. It just will not be as desirable for many. Of course if the general wins the war we accept his totalitarian leadership. If the Chinese one child policy allows for a more economically satisfying life for the Chinese we may accept it. If the Pope blesses us for following his commands, we are relieved—and joyous.

"As people who believe in the idea of democracy, we don't like the idea of totalitarian governance. We want to be able to decide on our personal lives."

"That's true Lee, but sometimes, especially in emergency situations, we are required to follow such a totalitarian type of regime because it is more efficient. It may or may not be a good idea but it will happen more quickly and completely when totally controlled from the top. When the totalitarian Chinese communists initiated the one child per family policy it generated a great deal of resistance from people who wanted more children, but it certainly is easing population growth in China and therefore in the world. It is probably, at least partially, responsible for the Chinese economic miracle. On the other hand the eventual problems of the increase of older people relative to younger and the increased number of males to females will also cause some social problems.

"But what were the alternatives? More people, more pollution, a lower standard of living, and a benefit to the rest of the human race because of this. It took a totalitarian approach to do this in a less developed country like China. As it becomes more developed and richer, child limitation may become voluntary, as in Europe and Japan. Ray, do you think the Catholic Church would function as well if it were democratically run than it is now with an all-powerful totalitarian leader?"

"I think that we all recognize that strong central leadership is swifter than consensus. Because of its potential speed it is often more effective and efficient than a parliamentary body. And of course we believe that the Pope has a pretty direct line to God, so he is less likely to make a mistake. Lee, one of the people in my parish did some legal research on the rights of parents. I brought some notes on a couple of cases. In Pierce v School Sisters (17) the state of Oregon was not allowed to require that all children be forced to take their first eight years of education in public schools. This seems to give parents some rights. What rights do parents actually have?"

"Ray, that was a 1925 case. It resulted in the rise of private school offerings, both religious schools and non-religious schools. That right certainly is generally accepted now."

"My parishioner also found the case of Wisconsin v Yoder (18) ruled that parents did not have to have their children in school."

"Well that's not exactly the ruling, Ray. It was a case of Amish parents not wanting their children to have to continue in the state's school system after the eighth grade. The children still went to public school for their first eight years."

"He also cited a California case (19) in which the judge said 'The family is the basic unit of our society, the center of personal affections that ennoble and enrich human life. It channels biological drives that might otherwise become socially destructive; it ensures the care and education of children in a stable environment; it establishes continuity from one generation to another; it nurtures and develops the individual initiative that distinguishes a free people.' I think that statement shows the importance of the family, at least in California."

"Ray, what the judge said is what we all want to believe. However he was ruling on a divorce, which under California law at that time was difficult to grant because severe wrongdoing had to be proven. The idea at that time was to preserve the marriage, no matter what. A few years later California law was changed to the "no fault" principle. So while the judge's words are well taken, they have nothing to do with California law today. As you well know, laws can be changed and judicial interpretations of laws can change. Even the Supreme Court reverses itself or qualifies earlier decisions.

"There is no legal right or obligation to have children in the United States. Legally a state might require licensing parents but it would probably have to show a 'compelling state interest' to overcome guaranteed freedoms, such as religion. Since the Declaration of Independence is not a law you couldn't use "the pursuit of happiness" as a legal reason for having children. And the Constitutional guaranty in the Fifth Amendment of protecting "life, liberty and property" wouldn't cover parenthood today. In older times when children, and wives, were 'property' it might have applied. Probably states could enact parent licensing laws under the Constitutional requirement 'to promote the general welfare' of the country. That would seem to be the best legal reason."

"That's informative Lee. But Wreck, I have been wondering how are you going to confront those who are skeptical to your ideas. It seems to me that you have to go back beyond the overpopulation problems to other issues such as global warming and the lack of water and land. It's not as simple as just saying there too many people. The question is 'why are there too many people?' I think you're going to have to confront the skeptics on global warming, on the space available for living, on how many people the planet could really handle, and such other issues or the uninformed people are just going to doubt you. Unless you can prove that the world is overpopulated and that is a threat to the survival of the race you're not going to get very far. In fact I think you're going to have to bring it down to the individual today and his or her interests. So I think you better look at the skeptics and what they will say and how you will counter them.

"Commander, if you are going to use reason and intelligence to get people to understand the problem, you must first tear down the faulty arguments. In general, skeptics seem to attempt to cast doubt on every issue. Some may want war more than peace, others want peace more than war. Some issues seem to develop more skeptics. It seems that the more an idea challenges the status quo or one's self-centered desires or hopes, the more skeptics enter the fray and the louder their voices. But as Herbert Spencer warned us 'There is a principle which is a bar against all information, which is proof against all arguments and which cannot fail to keep a man in everlasting ignorance -- that principle is contempt prior to investigation.'"

"I think that there are many people with a lot of knowledge who don't know how to use it. They may have a great deal of knowledge but they haven't put it together in a way that makes sense. I think that being wise is the combination of knowledge plus experience. A truly wise person knows how to use his or her knowledge for both enjoyment and for the good of humanity. But you are right Chet, I'm going to have to bring more knowledge to bear and hope that I can make people wiser and more thoughtful of the issues."

" So many times I have heard that wisdom begins only when we ask 'why.' We really need to question everything. For many millennia didn't everyone believe that the earth was flat? With better knowledge intellectuals realized that it was round. And with better measurements scientists found there was a little bit flat on the top and bottom, so it's not round, it's an oblate spheroid. Then with education, knowledge was spread to nearly everybody. Then that knowledge was used by the airline industry to fly shorter routes by heading north and flying a circular path, rather than a straight line between cities. So knowledge first had to occur and be verified, then it had to be generally disseminated, then it became useful to commerce."

"So what you're saying Ray, is that opinions and faulty knowledge can be changed. So maybe what we need are the Internet, computers and ways to teach reading and writing more effectively and more universally. It's clear that people can't make intelligent decisions if they don't have effective knowledge.

"It's not only true of the general population but our legislators also need to know more about physics and biology, laws should be based on facts not uninformed opinions. If we can't agree on the best facts, how can we make intelligent policies. So we need to get the best facts to the people. There will always be people with loud and colorful language and voices of authority, either their own or of a more authoritative but equally uninformed person—like a priest, bishop, legislator, radio commentator, or journalist.

CONFRONTING SKEPTICS ON GLOBAL WARMING

"There has been so much talk about warming that maybe this is the first place I should start to attack the skeptics. A recent survey of a number of countries showed that 40% of the people were willing to increase their taxes by 1% or more to help to reduce warming. On the other hand a third of the people were not willing to do anything. Russia was actually the worst with only 14% willing and 62% unwilling. The US was pretty much average with nearly 50% willing to pay 1% or more in taxes. That was pretty close to France, Japan, Mexico, Iran, Senegal, Kenya and Indonesia. The countries most willing to pay that extra 1% were China with nearly 70% and Vietnam at 60%. You would think that with as much as we know about climate change and the devastating effects it will undoubtedly have on our world that well over 95% would be willing to give far more than the 1% asked in this study.

"Climate science has for many years recognized the increase in the temperatures of the world even though we were supposed to be in a period of reducing temperatures. Actually we were in what was called a mini ice age, which ended with the beginning of the Industrial Revolution in the mid-18th century. In more recent years it had been hypothesized that greenhouse gases would reflect the Earth's heat back toward the land and that warming would result. Naturally people do not want to accept any facts that would upset them.

"In the latter part of the last century the concern about global warming became recognized. Businesses, particularly the coal and oil industries, felt that they had to do what they could to quiet the clamor. After all, if the energy industries were responsible for much of the warming, they might be heavily taxed or be required to clean up their production of energy sources. Think tanks, funded by business interests, quickly looked for evidence that could be used to counter the strong scientific evidence being disseminated. As you can imagine, when you are predicting things with a global perspective, there will be exceptions and questionable evidence that will pop up from time to time.

"Since overpopulation, and the advanced technology that the people of the planet are using, are the causes of climate change—and eliminating climate change is a nearly universal concern among informed people—perhaps we should first inform the skeptics of the imminent dangers of the reality. While we understand that the selfish interests of some oil producers are funding propaganda to question the unquestionable scientific facts—I guess we must start here if people are to understand the dangers of overpopulation to themselves and to their progeny

COMMON ARGUMENTS OF CLIMATE SKEPTICS

"Skeptics may say that yesterday was a cold day so global warming is not a fact. But the world is a big place and the overall temperature of the world is increasing. If you were to go into any room in your house and measure the temperature next to an external wall or on the floor or on the ceiling you would find differences in temperature. And your house is a small enclosed area. You can expect that a whole planet is going to show many divergences in temperature on a given day or in a given year. What needs to be done is to look at the overall temperature increase in the water and on land, at the equator and at the poles, on the mountain tops and in the deserts.

"Another survey showed relatively fewer scientists and engineers agreeing on global warming. As you might expect there was a difference in the opinions of the people in the different geological disciplines. The climatologists who were active in climate research showed that 97% agreed that humans play a role in global warming. But with petroleum geologists only 47% agreed. We might wonder if their connection with the petroleum industry might have influenced their opinions. On the other hand since it is the climatologists who research and publish in the area and should know more about long-term climate change, there was almost no disagreement about humans' contributions to global warming. It isn't surprising that those who know most about an area may have the most informed opinions.

HEMISPHERIC DIFFERENCES

"One such bit of evidence is related to comparing the Southern Hemisphere with the Northern Hemisphere. In the Southern Hemisphere there is far more water than land so any rise in temperature would be minimized by its absorption into the water. Some skeptics have used this variation as proof that the world is not warming. Of course it's not proof because we have to take the world as a whole. Naturally the climate scientists knew this, in fact it was their research that the skeptics were using. Every area of the world, every climate and sub-climate is going to react somewhat differently. One area may have an average temperature increase of 1° in the decade while another might actually cool. But it is the world, taken as a whole, that is being measured.

"As an example, Antarctica is colder than the polar regions in the north. In fact there are some areas of Antarctica that are actually gaining ice. But then there are other areas that are losing ice. So some people criticized the idea that the whole globe is warming because it was not warming as fast in the south. Then critics emphasized cold spells whenever they occurred, not telling their listeners that there was a big difference between weather and climate. Weather is the day-to-day and even year-to-year temperatures, while climate is the long-term accumulation of weather patterns."

" So here is a good example of propaganda being used by businesses and business related politicians. I often laugh at the special interest 'think tanks' that put out their propaganda. The Cato Institute is one that comes to mind. It calls itself a libertarian think tank, but it is funded by business, like the Koch brothers, and pro-marijuana groups. So their supposedly libertarian slant is more than a bit biased because of its financial backers. I have also seen a number of pro-Catholic web sites that push their agenda. Many of these sites will not allow dissenters to disagree. Some refuse to allow comment, others allow comment then screen them so that those who disagree are not allowed to have their comments printed.

WEATHER STATIONS

"Whenever skeptics try to prove their points they will look for any bits of evidence that exist that may counter the facts they are fighting. As an example, there areat various times between 3,000 and 14,000 weather and temperature reporting stations across the world. It would be unlikely they would all report identical temperatures. One American weatherman researched some of the American stations and found abnormal environments, such as: them being placed near heat sources. For example, if a thermometer is placed near an air conditioning outlet the air would be warmer at that point. Similarly if the thermometers are placed in cities we would expect them to record higher temperatures than those placed in nearby rural areas because the tarred roads of the cities, being black, will absorb more heat than would a green pasture. Similarly, concrete buildings will release more stored heat during the nighttime hours than would a farmhouse.

"To expect that the entire Earth would show uniform warming during every hour of the day would be far less likely than expecting all of the children in a school yard to be performing identical physical actions at the same time during their recess. But with the overwhelming evidence for warming, the occasional bouts of skepticism are soon overcome by the sea of evidence for those whose minds are open. So while public opinion may occasionally become skeptical, their ignorance of hope may soon be replaced by the reality of fear. Daily news reports of accelerated warming in different parts of the world hammer into our brains the information that the threat is real. But in our country people don't seem to get as much information as they do in a country like the UK. Media sources, like Fox News television, give a great deal of misinformation. Even the New York Times doesn't report on warming and environmental issues as much as the British papers. If you check most of our newspapers you will see that the major topics are world and local news along with sports and entertainment. In fact it seems that sports are our major concern. If you check the European newspapers you will often get 'environment' as a major topic. And you will usually have more comments by various journalists. The European papers are much more comprehensive and appeal to a more educated readership then do our American papers."

GREENHOUISE CAUSES AND EFFECTS

"I find that to be quite true Chet. But Wreck, what about skeptics and the effects of greenhouse gases?"

"While there are some people who don't acknowledge to reality of global warming, there are even more who don't acknowledge our human contributions to it. I haven't found any of these skeptics who have looked at the science of the problem.

"It doesn't take a genius to realize that greenhouse gases are produced by us humans and that since we have more humans using more energy from fossil fuels we are increasing warming. Add to that the fact that forests are being destroyed so that carbon dioxide cannot be absorbed by the diminishing plant world. The skeptics who are intelligent should look at the evidence. We don't expect the energy producing businesses or their paid propagandists, like their 'think tanks' to be swayed by the overwhelming evidence because their interests are not in understanding the truth but in amassing profits.

"While in the 20th century warming alone accounted for a degree or so of the global temperature increase, the estimates for the 21st century are that warming will rise 1 to 6 1/2° Celsius. If the skeptics will only believe the measurements made by important government agencies, like NASA, the National Climate Data Center, and by the universities, in terms of the warming of the land and the oceans, of the increased volumes of the oceans because warmer water expands, and of the numerous signs of northern hemisphere warming such as the earlier thawing and the later freezing of the ice flows near the North Pole, the skeptics might become believers. As in so many other areas of our lives, the comfort of inertia is preferable to any movement into the unknown—especially if that unknown is potentially very harmful. And what will happen to our earth and our descendants is certainly a major factor to consider. But undoubtedly the energy companies have a lot to lose if they are blamed for producing fuels that are causing the global warming. They spend a lot of money trying to convince the public and attempting to influence legislators to see it their way. I guess here we see the political techniques of not only producing propaganda but also of using the greed of legislators to change their behaviors.

"But let's go beyond the propaganda and look at the science. NASA scientists have assumed that 350 parts per million of CO_2 is the maximum allowable level. We passed that level a long time ago, in 2010. And now in 2025 we are well over 400 parts per million of CO_2. Every year the amount of carbon dioxide increases by 1 to 2 parts per million in the atmosphere. This may not seem like much but it represents millions of tons of carbon dioxide—70 million tons a day. To begin to reduce the level of atmospheric carbon dioxide we need to cut about 80% of our emissions. But governments are generally asking for only 20% to 50% cuts. This is obviously not enough to stop warming. So every year the temperature sets new high records.

"Then there is the matter of deforestation. Obviously the reduction of forests increases the amount of CO_2. Brazilian forests and Indonesian forests are being reduced by more than 1% per year. Some will say that there is so much air and so much water to absorb any CO_2 that we produce that reducing forests is not a factor in any climate change."

"Let me ask a couple of questions that I have heard mentioned relative to any human input into this global warming. First the carbon dioxide only stays in the atmosphere for about 10 years, so why worry?"

"That's true, but every generation puts more carbon dioxide into the atmosphere every year. And as our population increases we continue to get more atmospheric carbon dioxide remaining."

"What about the ocean being able to absorb huge amounts of this carbon dioxide?"

"We have talked about the limited amount of carbon dioxide that can be absorbed. Some of that becomes an acid in the water making the water more acidic. It also warms the water. And as the water warms its acidic content becomes more active and affects sea life. Carbonic acid (H_2CO_3) is formed when carbon dioxide and water interact.

I remember reading that the ocean hasn't been monitored long enough to be able to say that the acidification is any worse today than any time before."

"Well, my information from the oceanographic Department at the University of Southampton is that they are coring into polar ice and are able to go back millions of years to determine the acid level of the oceans and the amount of sea life that may have been destroyed when the acid levels were higher. So Ray I think you were reading a skeptical article that did not give you all the facts."

"What about this? It's been much hotter in previous times, such as medieval times in Europe. That was long before humans started using fossil fuels.

"The warming that happened in Europe around 1000 years ago was pretty much limited to Europe. It was not a global phenomenon."

" I know you talked about coring into the ice in the Arctic areas, I've heard that's not really good science because the carbon dioxide in the little air bubbles in the ice can escape and give imperfect measurements."

"That's true sometimes, but samples like this are taken all over the world and when compared to other measurements like tree rings we have a very accurate picture of the history of global temperatures and of the CO_2 presence in the atmosphere. Ray, you might be referring to measurements taken in the Arctic at Siple where it showed that before 1900 there was a CO_2 level of almost 330 parts per million, most of the scientists say it was only about 290 parts per million at that time. It's possible that at Siple there was an unusually high level of CO_2 for a month or a year. You have to understand Ray that these scientific findings are not based on a single instance. There are thousands of measurements and projections that indicate clearly that global warming exists. It is the skeptics and the single instances, such as you have just brought up, that attempt to counter the large amount of evidence that exists."

" Okay, here's the last one. We've had a lot of warming cycles in the past, tell me they were caused by carbon dioxide."

"In the past temperature fluctuations were not the result of carbon dioxide being produced by humans. Many things can affect temperature-- closeness to the sun, imbalances in the Earth's rotation and so forth. When these happened carbon dioxide was released from carbon sinks, like frozen flora and fauna near the poles that thawed because of the heat, it entered the atmosphere and you did get the greenhouse effect. But today it is carbon dioxide emitted by us that is causing the warming. So in the past the increased carbon dioxide was the result of warming from other factors, then the resulting greenhouse effect increased it. Today our problem is that carbon dioxide comes first, it is not a secondary reaction to other causes of warming. So the greenhouse effect comes without any other cause of warming.

GREENHOUSE GASES

"If we want to tie in global warming with overpopulation we can try looking at a country's total carbon emissions but it doesn't tell the full story of the country's contribution to global warming. China, for example, is the world's 'leader' in total emissions at 6018 million metric tons of carbon dioxide. It overtook the US, with its 5900 million metric tons, in 2007. But all that really tells you is that China is a fast-developing country with a lot of people. A more useful measurement is carbon emissions per person.

Under that measurement, the average American is responsible for 17.6 tons, while the average Chinese citizen is responsible for 6.2 tons.

"When we look around the world we see quite different amounts of carbon dioxide per person. For example, the average Australian emits 20.5 tons and the average person in the UK is at almost 10 tons. But in Kenya the average person's output is only a third of a ton. In India average person puts out just over a ton per year. South Africa is about the same as the UK, while Mexico is only about half that much. The oil-producing countries tend to be pretty high, with Saudi Arabia at 15 tons, Kuwait at 30 tons and Qatar at 60 tons. And just about every country is increasing its contribution per person annually.

"More people, even if the per capita emissions don't change, create a compounding effect of warming on our planet. That is why the outstanding faculty at the State University of New York's College of Environmental Science and Forestry, a premier environmental university department, has determined that overpopulation is our major environmental problem. Global warming was second. (19a)

"As we have said, the continuing emission of a number of gases into the atmosphere from human activities, including chlorofluorocarbons, or as we abbreviate them CFCs, methane, and, most important, carbon dioxide, is now a near certainty, if not a certainty, that it is creating a greenhouse effect and is putting the planet in jeopardy. Of course a major greenhouse gas is water vapor. The more the other gases create warming, the more water vapor can be held in the air. So it's not just carbon dioxide or the methane alone. Each one has a multiplying effect on warming beyond what it actually contributes.

METHANE

Methane has been increasing in the atmosphere rapidly in recent years. Whether this is because of more cattle and sheep being raised to feed the increasing number of people or whether it is the result of permafrost melting because of the warming, we don't know for certain. The permafrost across Russia and Canada is releasing great amounts of methane as the warming heads north and frozen animals and vegetables release their carbon and methane content. Add this to the methane produced from our waste in landfills and in the burning of waste, along with petroleum, coal and natural gas production. So we have an increase in a major greenhouse gas. As population increases more energy is needed, more food is needed, and more waste is produced-- all of which add to our warming.

CURRENT WARMING

The 2000 year cooling cycle, often called the Little Ice Age, ended in 1850 when the advancing Industrial Revolution really began human warming. The Little Ice Age was caused by a wobble in the Earth's axis of rotation which increased the Earth's distance from the Sun during the Arctic summer.

"Recently there have been temperatures that are far below normal in England and even Norway as well as in the eastern United States but at the same time there were higher than normal temperatures on the West Coast of the US. But this is all weather—not climate. Then, of course, natural phenomena can affect the weather.

"The volcanic eruption in Iceland in 2010 caused parts of the world to cool because the volcanic dust blocked out some of the sun's rays. But these changes are not related to climate change unless they persist for many years and affect the whole planet.

"In spite of the local ups and downs there is no doubt that global warming is speeding up. It is very likely that the upward trend in hot extremes and heat waves will continue. The duration and intensity of droughts have increased over greater areas since the 1970s, particularly in the tropics and subtropics. The Sahel area below the Sahara, the Mediterranean, southern Africa and parts of southern Asia have already become drier during the 20th century. (20) We have suffered from droughts here in California too, as you well know.

"It is particularly notable in the Arctic where ice is melting and where the exposed ground, which once reflected light back out to the atmosphere when it was covered with ice, now absorbs the heat. And these ice sheets, particularly the West Antarctic and the Greenland ice sheets, are melting faster than we thought. This should raise the sea level faster than expected, possibly as much as four feet in the century."

"The records of Arctic temperatures for the last 2000 years show that the first decade of this century was the warmest ever. And each year gets warmer. Without the human activity, the Arctic areas would have been about 1.4 degrees Celsius cooler than they have been recently. During the 20th century Arctic temperatures increased about three times faster than the rest of the Northern Hemisphere."

"I remember reading about 15 years ago that all of the 15 warmest years on record had come in the previous 20 years. And it wasn't just the thermometer talking. Hurricanes were getting stronger. We know that winter ice coverage of the Great Lakes has been reducing almost 1% per year over the last few decades. The Arctic and Antarctic ice caps are melting much faster than normal."

"Temperature records began to be kept in 1870. In recent years temperature collection has become more sophisticated. In addition to the worldwide temperature collecting stations, which number over a thousand, there are data on surface sea temperatures from satellites and there are the Antarctic research station measurements. These are analyzed by the Goddard Institute for Space Studies for NASA. Each decade since the 1980s has become warmer by about one-fifth of a degree Celsius. If we look back at the first decade of this century we find that 2005 was the warmest year with the following two years being tied for the second warmest year of all-time. If we look at the hemispheric differences, while 2005 was the warmest year on record for the northern hemisphere, 2009 was the warmest for the southern hemisphere. In the north, in 2008, there was a cooling trend due to a strong La Niña effect over the Pacific Ocean, but as it dissipated temperatures in the north regained their upward momentum.

"Pressure differences can also make a difference in the weather in large parts of the world. In 2009 a high-pressure system in the Arctic disrupted normal east-west flow of the jet stream causing cold air from the Arctic to move south in North America. This cooled North America but warmed the Arctic.

"American skeptics often cite cooler temperatures in some of their states as evidence of global cooling. The 48 contiguous states of the US account for only one and a half percent of the world's surface, so extrapolating the world's temperature from yesterday's cold spell in Chicago misses the point entirely. Also criticizing the possible inaccuracies of tree ring dating does not change the fact that over the last 150 years there has been significant warming. (20a)

"Being familiar with the research would help the skeptics understand that most of the warmest years in history have occurred in the last 30 years. If the skeptics want to criticize the measurements of NASA perhaps they need to develop a program that is as extensive as that of NASA's. If they want to criticize temperature reports from the 1000+ monitoring stations perhaps they need to set up their own 1,000+ stations around the world. It's just not enough to take a few bits of minor information and criticize the major findings which are accepted by over 95% of the scientists who study the phenomena.

Having a doctor or lawyer or a weatherman criticize the huge amount of evidence without having an equally huge amount of evidence to counter it is anti-intellectual. But as a political tactic it may have a delaying action on a government making a major start on saving the planet."

"James Lovelock, the father of the Gaia theory, says that we can't stop global warming. Many of us will die but humanity will continue, he said, but with fewer people. Lovelock believes that what we are doing is too little and too late. He was particularly pessimistic about the 'cap and trade' idea, which will make money for a small group of people, but will not do anything about the real problem."

"You probably know that more than 90% of all life forms that have existed are now extinct. Why should we think that our human species should go on forever?"

"OK already! But Wreck, What do you know about the possible cooling effects of some atmospheric elements? I understand that ammonium sulfate particles can reflect heat back away from the Earth. The ammonia released from some agricultural activities such as from fertilizers and animal waste can combine with sulfur, such as is released when coal is burned. At least that's what I understood from some studies done at Harvard University." (21)

"That's true. The preliminary investigation results have been forwarded to the United Nations' IPCC for further investigation. If it is true, the computer models on warming would need to be changed. But it doesn't change the fact that warming is occurring. It may only indicate why it is not occurring faster.

"I don't know if you read the United Nations report based on an analysis of 400 peer-reviewed scientific studies that projected there would be a 6°C rise in temperature by the end of this century if we don't make severe cuts in our emissions. They went on to say that if the US and Western Europe cut their emissions by 80% and the developing world cut theirs by 50% the increase might only be 3°."

I'm sure you are all familiar with the intergovernmental project on climate change which brings together the world's leading climate scientists and experts. It concluded that major advances in climate modeling and the collection and analysis of data now give scientists very high confidence, at least a 9 out of 10 chance of being correct, in their understanding of how human activities are causing the world to warm. This level of confidence is much greater than the IPCC indicated in their last report in 2001. It is highly likely that humanity's emissions of carbon dioxide, methane, nitrous oxide and other greenhouse gases have caused most of the global temperature rise observed since the mid-20th century. The report said that the effect of human activity on the planetary temperature is five times greater than the effect of the sun's activity.

"Ice coring research gives us records going back 10,000 years. They show the dramatic increase in greenhouse gases from the time of the industrial revolution in 1750. An increase of about 3° Celcius, which is about 6° Fahrenheit, is expected this century. While the Earth's surface temperature has only risen 0.74°C, it should now rise about 0.2°C per decade.

"Some climate skeptics point to the increased snowfall on the eastern seaboard in 2010 as evidence that global warming was not occurring. But the fact is that climate scientists had already confirmed that more rain and snow could be expected because of warming. Over the last few decades the amount of water vapor in the air has increased by 4%. I understand that that is about 500,000,000 tons of water. It comes from evaporation from oceans, lakes and reservoirs, from water used in irrigation, from the burning of fossil fuels-- which all break down into various amounts of carbon dioxide and water, and from other industrial factors. So with the increase in water vapor you can understand how when the weather does cool down there is more vapor in the air and the cooler air can't handle as much water as warmer air, so it comes down in the form of rain or snow.

”Well if water vapor is helping to raise the temperature, why does it get cool?”

”There are lots of other things that affect weather. The flows of cold or warm air and the shifting of high and low pressure areas greatly affect the day-to-day weather. So does the length of the day. In winter in the Northern Hemisphere the days are shorter so there is less sunlight per 24-hour period, consequently less heat from the sun can arrive on the Earth's surface. Of course the lower angle of the winter sun also reduces the amount of heat landing on the northern hemispheric land. Then there is the El Nino effect which arises in the Pacific Ocean every few years. It brings more moisture to the West Coast and the southern US and increases the rainfall there. But it also can affect the jet streams pushing them eastward and southward and increasing the rain, snow, and cold weather further east and south. The increased warmth near the Great Lakes increases the evaporation of the water so that more water in the atmosphere will create heavier snows. But in the long run with more warming, it will become rain rather than snow. So there are many influences on the weather. The greenhouse gases are only part of the equation--but a very important part.

"You probably know about water vapor being about twice as powerful a greenhouse gas as carbon dioxide. But the amount of water vapor increases as the temperature increases from the greenhouse effect of the other gases such as carbon dioxide and methane. For every degree Celsius that the temperature warms, water vapor is increased by 6 to 7.5%. So any atmospheric warming caused by greenhouse gases increases the warming even more through the increase in water vapor.

"It's really very complicated, but like my old professor said 'if you don't know everything you don't know anything.' Certainly the climate scientists are closer to knowing everything while the deniers are closer to not knowing anything. When you have the big business people, like the coal and oil companies, putting huge amounts of money into think tanks like the Cato Institute, you can expect strong denials but no solid evidence to back their claims. It's politics versus science. The short-term interests of business versus the long-term survival of the people on the planet.”

"It's like what we talked about when we were talking of propaganda, people who can gain by pooh-poohing the idea of climate change will look to find any twig that they can make others believe is a tree. When the scientists who are most involved in the research on global temperature, like the climatologists, are held to be inferior to the desires of business interests or religious ideals we have a problem. In the US a recent survey of over 3000 scientists involved in the study of climate found 99% agreed that human activity was a cause of global warming. (22)

"But presidential aspirant Sarah Palin called all of the scientific evidence 'snake oil', referring to the nostrums that quacks in the 1800s used to sell as elixers that could cure anything. Of course she didn't cite any evidence to counter the massive evidence on the other side. But then politicians don't need evidence when they are preaching to their choirs.”

PROBLEMS ON LAND

"You know that, the warming increases the warming. By that I mean as forests and shrubbery become drier and more likely to be fuel for forest fires. Forest fires not only destroy the carbon dioxide consuming plants and trees but they release carbon into the air from the trees that burn, so they further increase the problems of warming. So one thing increases the actions of other things.

" The destruction of forests to find more agricultural land, to find more wood for building and for paper production accounts for about 20% of the CO_2 increase in the atmosphere. 20% of the world's CO_2 is attributable to deforestation. So it's not just our cars and trucks that are the problem."

" You have probably been keeping up with the reports from California showing that wildfires should increase, water will be reduced, and crop lands will be lost because of the lack of water.

"Those wildfires are really scary. When I was growing up in Malibou Lake we seemed to have a fire about every seven years. Then the time between the fires kept reducing and the fires became more severe. For the last 20 years I've followed the fires in California and other places and they seem to be much more frequent and much more disastrous than in the past. And think of the fresh water they use to fight the fires. It is a double ecological negative, destroying trees and homes and using water.

POLAR ICE CAPS

"Let's go from hot to cold. Every year we see that the polar ice caps are melting faster than we expected and oceans are rising faster than the United Nations had projected just a few years ago. The Greenland ice sheet is losing 180 billion tons of ice a year. Arctic sea ice has shrunk almost 3% per decade since 1980.

"Snow cover in most areas has reduced about 7% in the Northern Hemisphere in the latter half of the 20th century. At the same time the freezing dates of the ground and rivers is about six days later per century, while the thawing dates are six days earlier per century. This translates to about a one day per decade change in freezing. (23)

"Another factor, just recently investigated, is that as the ice melts and land is exposed, the land absorbs more heat which contributes to more global warming. While the globe has warmed about 0.8 degrees, about 1.4 degrees Fahrenheit, the polar regions have heated more than the lower latitudes. University of Michigan research shows that since 1978 there has been a 14% reduction of heat reflected back into space--from 3.75 to 3.3 watts per square meter of snow covered area. This 14% reduction in reflected heat becomes a 14% increase in warming from that area.

"This ice melting, particularly ice that was over the land, along with the warming of the oceans may make the ocean level rise by a meter in the next 75 years. Ocean temperatures have been increasing 50% faster than had been predicted just 5 years ago.

"Predictions often miss the mark, even if they're on the right track. For example, one prediction was that the Himalayan glaciers would disappear by 2035. The truth is they will disappear but it probably won't be as early as 2035. This earlier prediction was jumped on by the skeptics as soon as the date was revised. This is a problem for science in that all of the variables can never be known. So science deals with probabilities, while skeptics jump on every new occasional misstep but they seldom do any research themselves.

"But back to the Himalayas. As they disappear the people in southwest China and other areas will be wanting for water. The Swiss-based United Nations World Glacier Monitoring Service has been monitoring more than 200 glaciers since 1950. They have found that they are reducing significantly-- far faster than before. The temperatures in the Himalayas are expected to rise 5 or 6° over the next century. The global warming is increased in the Himalayas by black soot falling on the snow and making it more heat absorbent. The soot comes from the cooking fires of the nearby people as well as the burning of kerosene, diesel oil, and coal. The point is that the glaciers are melting, and more important they will affect the rivers that they feed and the farms that the rivers feed. This will severely affect how the people who depend on this food will feed themselves.

THE OCEANS

"Ocean scientists find large areas of water, both lakes and oceans, with less than the normal amount of oxygen because it has been starved out with the absorption of carbon dioxide by that water. This has the dual result of interfering with the fish food chain and with the release of nitrous oxide which is another greenhouse gas that will increase alarmingly and will lead to less food being produced and quite probably to more human cancers. Another factor that we talked about earlier, is the rising sea level due to the increased warmth of the ocean which increases its volume. Then add the water from the melting glaciers and ice caps throughout the world and you get a significant expansion of the existing ocean water.

"Some areas are already experiencing problems from the rising water. China's rise in sea level over the last several decades has averaged 2.6 millimeters a year while the global average for the rise in sea level has been 1.7 millimeters. But last year the average rise was 8 millimeters, and in Hainan it was 113 millimeters. Elsewhere in China the ocean temperature went up to 28.5°Celsius, the second highest temperature on record and the sea level went up 180 millimeters. So obviously not every part of the world experiences the same rise in sea level simultaneously. Predictions are that some coastal areas could face rises of over a meter per decade. This of course will result in some loss of farmland and the salinization of other land. The rise in water level will undoubtedly force people from their homes. The first to be forced from their homes by rising seas were some people in the islands near New Guinea. That was in 2010.

"Seventy percent of the world's population live on coastal plains and 11 of the world's 15 largest cities are on coasts or estuaries. Researchers at Oxford University have said that a 2 meter rise in sea level is now almost unstoppable. Even if we were able to hold warming to 2° Celsius this century, the sea level would rise from 1/2 to 1 1/2 meters. (24)

"Sea levels have been rising 80% faster than they were predicted to rise in 2001. In the 2001 UN report it was estimated that the sea level rise would be between 9 and 88 cm. The newer report has narrowed the estimates to between 28 and 58 cm. however if the ice sheets continue to melt as temperature rises, it could rise another meter. (25)

"As in other areas of life, predictions can go either way. How many divorced people thought that it would happen to them on their wedding day? How many people thought they would lose their houses when the economy was going well in the early part of this century

"But that's not the end of the problems for the oceans. A number of studies from universities and other scientific groups have shown huge increases in the acidity of water of the oceans. As you probably know carbon dioxide and water form carbonic acid. A recent series of studies between Hawaii and Alaska have shown huge increases in carbonic acid since 1991. These changes occurred down to about 1/2 mile of ocean depth. The ocean seems to be absorbing about 30% of the man-made carbon dioxide. The problem is that even if we stopped our production of carbon dioxide the effects in the ocean would probably last at least 1000 years. The acidity of the oceans affects the food chain and the ability of shellfish to make their shells. By about 2050 the acidity of the ocean will have doubled from the level of the pre-Industrial Revolution days.

CHANGING WEATHER PATTERNS

"As has been clarified before, climate and weather mean two different things. Climate is the overall general level of sun, cold, and precipitation. It can be rated for the whole world, for a nation, or even for a city. The weather is the more fleeting short-term fluctuations in heat and cold, rain and snow. Weather is happening today or it happened within the last year or so. Climate has been happening over a very long period of time. The fact that at the 2010 Olympics in Vancouver the weather was unseasonably warm does not prove that global warming exists. At the same time the unseasonably cold weather along the eastern seaboard with snow in Florida, did not prove that global warming did not exist. That was all weather. The world's climate was still warming."

"With nearly 100% of the experts agreeing that the world is warming and that it will have dire consequences for us all, why are those without scientific knowledge allowed to push their unscientific opinions on the rest of us. I guess we go back to inductive logic and hoping that the facts will make people think. Why is it that the leaders of the world and the scientists involved are saying that there is a huge problem, but the business interests are pushing their political buttons to make so many people doubt the hard evidence?"

"It seems that the lack of education in the world coupled with our instinct to deny that anything bad will happen, or that things could change tomorrow, holds us back from recognizing the threat. I would hope that common sense will eventually get people to realize that global warming is happening and has been happening for over 100 years."

"But Wreck, common sense is quite uncommon, but even when it's there it is no good without some effective education. We need some science to go with that common sense. Remember common sense tells us that the world is flat. Common sense tells us that the heavy object will fall faster than a light object, as Aristotle assumed. But Galileo disproved this. So common sense was wrong again. Common sense tells us that the sky is blue. But science explains why it is colorless but it appears blue because of the way light rays are bent. Common sense tells us that the planets and the other stars are merely specks in the heavens. But astronomers have proven that most of those specs are far bigger than our world. So much for common sense. What we need is enough education to be able to comprehend what is happening in our world.

"You may have heard of Lord Stern of Brentford, the world's leading climate change economist. He concluded that, even if each country formally adopted the tightest targets in the ranges they had proposed before the Copenhagen Conference, the temperature would still rise more than 2 degrees Celsius. The world's leading economies had agreed to limit the increase to 2 degrees Celsius above the pre-Industrial Revolution levels to avoid the worst effects of climate change. Lord Stern said the world needed to cut emissions from 47 billion tons of CO_2, the predicted figure for 2010, to 44 billion tons by 2025. Lord Stern said that there was a gap of up to 5 billion tons between the cuts that the most ambitious targets would deliver and what was needed to reach 44 billion tons by 2025. As we know, it hasn't been done.

"Prior to the Copenhagen Conference our country was offering a 4% drop in CO_2 levels. Meanwhile the EU was offering 20% and was willing to go to 30% if other countries would also make similar sacrifices. Meanwhile China was dragging its feet for the same reason that the US was. Cuts in energy are bad for business. Today the average Chinese is emitting 6.3 tons of CO_2 on the average while the European rate is at 5.5 tons. Of course our American citizens are more than twice as bad as the Chinese citizens and nearly 3 times as bad as the Europeans, since we emit 17.6 tons per person.

"It's a shame that the world seems to follow us when we popularize a rock star, a movie idol, or even a disease. But we can't follow the world when it is doing a better job than we are."

"What do you mean 'popularizes a disease?'"

"Well, when Americans find that they are suffering an inordinate amount of depression, their symptoms are readily treated with a pill from one of the big pharmaceutical companies. If you can sell the pill in the U.S., why not in Japan, Italy, the UK and Indonesia?

"I'm not sure that today's people are more depressed than those who suffered through the Great Depression, the Dust Bowl or a divorce or death. The mind and body have usually been able to cope, given enough time. Of course with 'happy pills', both legal and illegal, being available –we are impatient and want relief instantly."

CONFUSING THE ISSUES

"Some years ago the governor of Virginia and his attorney general, two conservative lawyers without academic training in science, determined that the evidence for global warming was 'unreliable, unverifiable, and doctored' science and that believing in global warming would result in the loss of jobs. They were strongly countered by the professors at the University of Virginia in the Environmental Science Department and those of the Virginia Climatology Office.

"If we are looking at the rules of logic you would see that keeping jobs and recognizing climate change are two quite different areas. While it may be true that climate change recognition might someday reduce the mining of coal in the area, it might also increase the jobs in green science. So the use of this scare tactic as a political technique was used to throw off the reality of another kind of very real threat."

" I can't get over the fact that with the threat that we have, that people haven't taken the time to investigate it on their own rather than listening to business interests that are trying to cloud the evidence, not with facts, but with doubting and with political techniques that have nothing to do with the issue. If they are sincerely interested in disproving global warming, they need to work to try to disprove that: the world's climate has risen about 1°C in the last 125 years and that the world's greenhouse gases began increasing about 1850 along with the Industrial Revolution. Most of the warming in the last 50 years has been because of an increase in greenhouse gases. And if that's not enough, with the increasing rate of emissions, our future climate will change even more rapidly with more heat, more rains, and stronger hurricanes. Beginning in this century we certainly saw more serious snows and rain storms. Europe had several record-breaking floods and there were hurricanes and typhoons that were extremely strong. We could surmise that these were due to the effects of global warming, but we can't prove it. Maybe those skeptics could put the money into research and see if the research backs up their opinions. But of course there's a difference in researching to find out what is true and researching to find evidence that backs up your business interests."

"If it weren't so tragic it would be hilarious the way some of the 'denier' politicians like to use the word conspiracy. But what have climate scientists to gain from publishing their academic work? On the other hand what have the oil companies and coal companies to gain by keeping the legislators from imposing taxes on their operations? I have even heard that Al Gore is part of the conspiracy because he is making money on green energy projects. But he could've just as easily invested in oil stocks!

DISEASES AND NATURAL DISASTERS

"But there is more to worry about with temperature rises. With the increase in temperature more countries will be infected with mosquito borne diseases like Dengue Fever, malaria, Yellow Fever, West Nile virus, and some types of encephalitis. Dengue fever has spread from nine countries 50 years ago to 100 countries today including most of the United States.

"These communicable disease problems will probably go hand-in-hand with droughts and famines. It could certainly be expected also that we will find violence used as a tool to claim the land of others when we have lost ours to Neptune.

TREACHERY AMONG THE SKEPTICS

"You may remember back in about 2010 e-mails and documents from East

Anglia University were hacked by people in Turkey and Russia and selected mails or excerpts from a few mails were put on the Internet. A major issue was that the climate scientists were concerned with the skeptics. They showed a concern for keeping some of the research out of the hands of the skeptics. Some climate skeptics claimed that the e-mails fabricated research on the dangers of warming.

Both press and science organizations concluded no such thing from those e-mails. There was no question that warming existed and that human activities were largely responsible. The legitimate criticisms of the e-mails was that the few scientists involved felt that there was a need for some secrecy of their work and many had sought to control premature disclosure of it. There was nothing in the e-mails to indicate any falsification of evidence. And in fact the evidence produced at East Anglia and Penn State universities was consistent with the findings of researchers at other research institutes. While the skeptics used some phrases taken out of context to cast doubt on all climate research, thorough governmental investigations of the e-mails showed that there was no cover-up and that the research showed clearly that warming was occurring.

"In one e-mail an author mentioned the word 'trick' to indicate a technique used by another scientist to describe yearly temperature variations, using actual temperatures and other dating techniques like tree rings. The skeptics took the word 'trick' to mean deception, which was not the intent of the author. Here is another illustration of a text being taken from its context and being misinterpreted by someone without the ability to interpret.

"Another similar term taken out of context and misunderstood was the term 'hide the decline' which the skeptics took to mean hiding evidence, but the real meaning related to what climatologists had to do with temperature differences between actual measured temperatures and tree ring dating indications of temperatures which varied."

"Wreck, I can think of a few football terms that if taken out of context could certainly be misinterpreted. When we talked about 'headhunting' we were not talking about it in the sense that cannibals might, we were talking about making tackles. And when we talked about 'sky' and 'cloud' we were talking about responsibilities in pass coverages, not about what we might see when we looked up. And when we talked about 'dogs' we were talking about linebackers rushing the passer. So I guess it's pretty clear that when you take a term from one context and interpret it in another context you are certainly going to have semantic problems and your interpretations will be meaningless.

"When the tobacco companies hid or falsified evidence it didn't change the fact that people were dying from tobacco in large numbers. That was lying at the corporate level. "Then there is the common tactic of attacking a person rather than an argument that the person is making. So often the skeptics make fun of Al Gore, but they don't disprove his message. You remember our talk about logic, attacking a person rather than an argument is a logical fallacy.

EDUCATION IS ESSENTIAL TO MAKING PEOPLE SCIENTIFICALLY AWARE

"More than a third of the world has never heard of global warming.(26) While 99% of Japanese have heard of it and 97% of Americans had heard of it, only 15% of the people of Liberia were aware of it. And when the people were asked about the cost of global warming it was the Latin Americans who generally came out with the highest percentages. In fact of the top 20 countries where people said that human activity is responsible for much of global warming, 13 were in Latin America. South Korea showed the most awareness of global warming being a human product, with 92% of the people believing this. In the US, by contrast, only 49% said they thought the warming was a result of human activities."

"The internet should be your best way of educating people. Certainly it can be used for negative purposes, such as teaching terrorists how to make bombs, and attempting to get people to narrow their thinking into one ideological pigeonhole. It may be a recruiting tool for a religious sect or for a political movement without requiring the user to think his or her way to a rational conclusion. It can also be used as a force for good. And I think on balance, far more good than bad results from using the Internet. Some countries, like China, are censoring the Internet access. This can be seen as bad if you think that freedom of speech includes every aspect of one's freedom, such as access to child pornography or a terrorist bomb making. But I think the positive possibilities outweigh the negatives.

CONFRONTING SKEPTICS ON OVERPOPULATION

"Let's move to your major problem, the skeptics who doubts overpopulation. The propagandists lead the skeptics by often using condescending terms for those who say that there is an overpopulation problem. They may say it is a 'pop creed' or Malthusian. Ridicule is a way to make your followers feel superior to the people you are ridiculing. It can be an effective political technique for those who don't think.

"The skeptics may say that the Founding Fathers felt strongly for freedom. And naturally they extend that to having the freedom to have an unlimited number of children. Of course they didn't think that the voters should have the freedom to vote directly for their president. Their system of choosing electors has resulted in the country having 18 presidents who were not chosen by a majority of the voters. Two of them are commonly ranked among the top five presidents—Abraham Lincoln and Harry Truman. On the other hand three of those often are listed among the five worst—George W. Bush, James Buchanan and Benjamin Harrison. The 'Great Compromise' which allowed proportional representations in the House of Representatives, but two senators from each state did not give the larger states the freedom to influence treaties, Supreme Court appointments or such decisions as whether to go to war. California, with 60 times more people than Wyoming, has senators with equal legislative impact. The Founding Fathers who allowed gun possession in order to keep 'a well regulated militia' have had their intentions significantly changed by legislation and court decisions. The separation of church and state has been significantly altered with tax deductions for churches and the recognition of God in the Pledge of Allegiance and in many other areas of government. So assuming that some ideas relative to the idea of 'freedom' were held by the Founding Fathers, ever if we could accurately determine them, should direct our thinking today is not borne out by our laws and traditions today—since we have obviously moved counter to many of the ideas that they actually did have. And, none of the Founding Fathers ever expressed their opinions on global warming or overpopulation.

"With the intelligence of the Fathers we might assume that they would be well versed in the sciences if they lived today. They would probably therefore recognize what the top researchers in the world have determined about global warming.

"What the skeptics don't do is to look at the decreasing amount of arable land and fresh water. Both are limiting factors to living healthy lives. They never suggest a maximum population for the world—especially one that takes into consideration the real factors that relate to overpopulation, like the using up of many natural resources and the production of wastes such as heavy metals, plastics, nuclear wastes, et cetera. They deny global warming in spite of the overwhelming scientific evidence for it. They say that 'the population doomsayers have always been wrong' but they seldom mention any. They misconstrue the ideas of Malthus who was speaking to an England that at the time was self-sufficient in agriculture. Today they are net importers of food. They are only about 60% self sufficient in producing their food.(27) The skeptics have some legitimate criticisms of some of the predictions made by Paul Ehrlich in his book in the 1960s, but they can't criticize his basic message.

"It may not seem strange that their financing comes from businesses that would be hurt if population were to reduce. I have looked at the websites of their think tanks and have been appalled that they don't accept comments. Libertarian and conservative think tanks, such as the Cato Institute seem to speak with the authority of the Pope—getting their information directly from God or the oil companies."

"Even so, your skeptics need to be reminded that those who never change their opinions will never be able to correct their mistakes so they will never be any smarter than they once were, or thought they were. The open-minded people, particularly those with physical science backgrounds, should be able to understand the problems of global warming and the use of natural resources. People with medical or sociological backgrounds should be able to see the needs of better living through a reduced population and more concern for the children brought into the world. There's an old saying that 'a wise man can see more from the bottom of a well than a fool can see from a mountain top.' You will obviously have to clarify the visions for those fools on the mountain tops. You must give them intellectual binoculars."

"I know that your primary concern in reducing population is to reduce the global warming effect on the planet."

"That's a major reason. But there's also the need to have people in jobs throughout their lives. There is certainly a reason to try to keep jobs in the home countries of people rather than have them illegally migrating to other countries. There is the obvious need to keep people working longer in their lives rather than retiring in their 60s, so we won't need so many young people to take their places. There is a need to reduce poverty and to get all the world's people fed properly. And of course there's also the freshwater problem. But let's start looking at what the skeptics will be saying when I approach the need to control our population.

"It is unquestioned that more than 200,000 people are added daily to the world's population. It is unquestioned that fresh water is becoming more scarce. It is unquestioned that arable land per person is being reduced. It is unquestioned that global warming is a result of excess population. If only 10 1/2% of the world's land is arable, as the CIA has determined, then each baby born reduces the acreage for each person on earth. When we realize that part of the arable land is forest or jungle which is necessary to convert the carbon dioxide to oxygen, we have even less arable land per person. Yet we need more forest and jungle for every person born to reduce his carbon footprint.

"If we figure that today, in 2025, each person has less than half an acre of arable land, counting forests, we see that we have a problem. And when we see that the US and Europe have much more than the average arable land per person, we can understand that the people in the Mideast, Pakistan, Africa, and China have less."

"Commander, you should probably also point out that many of the people making the decisions about population, warming, and poverty live in the areas where arable land and water supplies are not so pressing. Northern Europe and northern America will be much less concerned because they haven't suffered from the famines and diseases that have afflicted those in most other parts of the world.

"True Chet. But I think they have to be convinced just as the Third World countries need to be. As we said earlier, the skeptics must be pushed to define their positions, such as how many people per arable acre of land is minimal or maximal. They need to define how much freshwater is needed per person. They need to be pushed to evaluate scientifically the issues related to overpopulation.

"Poverty, immigration, famines, disease and so forth are real. They may say that the problem with famine is that the food producing countries will not supply the poor countries or that it is transportation that is the problem in getting food to the hungry. They may say that ocean water can be desalinized but they neglect to say how it will be paid for. With the exception of Norway and one or two other countries, every country has a national debt. Which of the so-called rich countries are willing to go more into debt to pay for the desalinization of water for poorer countries? And where is that money going to come from? There is no great banker in the sky ready to loan every country what it needs at interest they can pay while servicing their existing national debts.

"If there were unlimited money, unlimited arable land, unlimited freshwater, and unlimited pollution free energy, maybe there wouldn't be the real problem that exists. I have yet to see any skeptics proposing real solutions to the problems of warming, poverty, illegal immigration and so forth. They may say that everyone in the world can fit comfortably into Texas, but they neglect to say that there isn't enough arable land or water in Texas to support them. If we gave one acre of land to everyone we could fit a little over one billion people into Texas. That would be about 14% of the world's population. But the arable land in Texas is only about 20% of the total land, so if we divided the arable land among the total population of the world each person would have about 125 square meters of land for their home, their farms, the land necessary to graze their cattle, and forests to convert their carbon dioxide back to oxygen. Then, of course, you would need roads, business buildings, and many other land using structures necessary for a civilization. Most people in the West have homes that are over 125 square meters, that's 1250 square feet. Additionally Texas has water problems so there wouldn't be nearly enough water to support the world's population.

"Then we might ask at what level of income should everyone live. If we all live at the level of the citizens of Mali we can support more people than if everyone lives at the level of Luxembourg."

"From what I've read the skeptics either just deny overpopulation without any evidence or they criticize people who in the past said that we were going to have overpopulation, like Thomas Malthus and Paul Ehrlich. We might as well criticize Aristotle for not having the knowledge of today's physicists when he suggested that a heavy object falls faster than lighter object. The theory of Malthus made great sense when it was proposed, his idea that humans grow exponentially while food production grows arithmetically seems to be only half true today. Genetically modified food, pesticides, fertilizers and academic knowledge about how to grow plants more effectively were not available to Malthus. Of course today we have other problems relative to growing food. Freshwater for irrigation is reducing considerably. The available arable land is decreasing as erosion and building eliminate over 200,000 square miles per year. Fertilizer components are reducing as they become more expensive. Mass production requires more oil, as does the transportation of the food.

"Skeptics may say that there is extensive literature critiquing the concept of human overpopulation. But they don't list the literature or any scientific studies and projections that might aid them in demolishing what they call the overpopulation myth. One writer that I read backed up his statement there was massive literature on his side gave as his evidence a science fiction story that he thought was poorly done. He did address an article by Russell Hopfenberg that postulated that population is limited when food is limited. But then the critic jumps to comparing the Western developed world with its reducing population to their availability to adequate food. Of course it wasn't Hopfenberg's thesis, in fact it was just the opposite. Obviously more than food can limit population. The ability of people in the developed world to choose whether or not to have children based on their self-centered interests is an entirely different matter. What Hopfenberg had written was that when food is not available people cannot survive. He was not talking about voluntary family planning.

"Rather than criticizing the idea that there are too many people in the world and that the overpopulation problem is getting worse, the skeptic criticized the idea that food relates to fertility. If you remember the logical fallacies from your university classes on logic, you can understand that this critic was setting up a 'straw man' and attacking an area which is not germinal to the proposition. He said he was arguing against the idea that there were too many people in the world.

"The skeptic never did attack the idea that there were too many people in the world, that they contribute to climate change, that they contribute to legal and illegal immigration to find jobs, that there is a major problem with supplying water, and so forth. Other skeptics merely quoted Genesis, which said that we must 'be fruitful and multiply.' And the pro-business critics usually don't offer any scientific arguments--just that it is bad for the economy to limit population and that technology will save us."

"I remember reading a blog on Earth Day about 15 years ago.(28) It seemed that the writer took the familiar approach that people's freedom is being threatened when overpopulation is addressed. I couldn't help thinking that if famine and global warming threaten large numbers of the population, that dead people are not going to profit very much from freedom. I think most of us would prefer life. Maybe Patrick Henry was an exception. Without citing any evidence, the blogger declared the concern with overpopulation was merely 'poppycock.'

"He used a common argument that I just mentioned that all the people in the world could fit into the state of Texas and have 100 square meters for themselves. Assuming they build a 1000 square foot house, which is not all that big, they would have no more room to grow the food they need, to park their cars, or any room to drive them. He didn't mention the fact that today the average person only has about a half an acre of arable land as his share of the world's arable land. As is common, these critics never think out the total problems of the world. They merely offer simplistic solutions that any unthinking person might accept.

"Then he criticized Paul Ehrlich's prediction in his book 'The Population Bomb' of 40 years earlier in which Ehrlich had predicted that people would starve en masse by the 1980s. The blogger either didn't know about, or was hiding the fact that, Ethiopia had huge famines in the 70s and 80s, as did the African Sahel, the area just south of the Sahara that extends all the away across Africa. You probably know that the Sahara is extending southward at up to 30 miles per year so the once arable land is becoming desert fast. Mr. Schiff may not consider it a famine when only a quarter of a million people die, as happened in the 80s in Ethiopia. As you remember, Wreck, that the Institute for Natural Resources in Africa predicted about that time that by today Africa would only be able to produce enough food for a quarter of its population. Schiff should have known about the 1980s famine in Karamoia, Uganda that killed over 20% of the population and 60% of the babies. In terms of mortality it was one of the worst famines in history. Nearly a million people died, but 6 million were saved by massive food donations from the West. Then in 2009 and 2010 a huge water related problem affected Niger, Chad, Nigeria and other areas. The international community was again called in to try to avert another famine. And of course there was the North Korean famine of the mid-90s that may have killed up to 3 million people. But naturally when you have an opinion that you want others to believe, you should not let facts stand in the way of your propaganda!

"Then he went on to criticize the legal battles of people trying to save different species of animals. Of course this has nothing to do with human overpopulation. It's a whole different issue. But I would agree that people should come before other animals. Still the point is that so often people who are trying to make one point cloud it with another—here again we have the 'straw man' fallacy we talked about earlier.

CHALLENGING THE MYTH OF OVERPOPULATION

"I heard a spokesman for the Foundation for Economic Education, one of the oldest free-market organizations in the United States.(29) It was founded to study and advance the freedom philosophy. Its mission is to offer the most consistent case for the 'first principles' of freedom: the sanctity of private property, individual liberty, the rule of law, the free market, and the moral superiority of individual choice and responsibility over coercion.

"Its spokesman said that these ideals have been ignored for far too long. We need to go back to the thinking of the Founding Fathers. In arguing that overpopulation is a myth he said that the prefix 'over' implies a standard. What is the optimum or ideal number of people of the world. 'For overpopulation to be real, there must be conditions that are undesirable and unmistakably caused by the presence of a certain number of people. If such indications cannot be found, we are entitled to dismiss the claim of overpopulation.' Maybe there are too few people in the world today. What are the requirements for the world to be overpopulated?

"Well I would come back with the question of what is either the maximum or the optional population. There certainly is famine, deepening poverty, disease, environmental degradation and depletion of natural resources. There is certainly a great deal of illegal immigration from countries that don't have enough work for their population. Central America, Southern Africa, the Mideast and other areas had people fleeing to the US, Europe and other areas. We might ask if people in their native country should have the freedom to work there at livable wages. I wonder what he would say to that?

"If you would look at each of these things that he just mentioned he could answer his own question. But we have here a person holding freedom above survival. If we don't survive what good is freedom, we'll all be dead!"

"He said that the television pictures of starving, emaciated Africans are heartbreaking, but they are not evidence of overpopulation. Since 1985, we have witnessed famine in Ethiopia, Sudan and Somalia. Those nations have one thing in common: They are among the least populated areas on Earth. Although their populations are growing, the people there are not hungry because the world can't produce enough food; they are hungry because civil war keeps food from getting to them. Moreover, the very sparseness of their populations makes them vulnerable to famine because there aren't enough people to support sophisticated roads and transportation systems that would facilitate the movement of food."

"Let me check my laptop. . . . . Here under WorldAtlas.com is a list of the population densities 192 countries. The most dense is Monaco with 42,000 people per square mile. Next comes Singapore and Malta. Somalia has about 35 people per square mile, they are number 169 of the 192 countries in the world. Sudan has 42 people per square mile so that makes them number 159. Ethiopia has 127 people per square mile and they are about midway in the list at 102.

"Ray, your source doesn't seem to recognize that food costs money and these are pretty poor countries. A good part of what they eat is donated to them. So somebody else is paying for it. He also seems to assume that all land is arable. It is not. I want to get into that in a few minutes so let's leave that for awhile."

"Then he said that in the 20th century there has been no famine that has not been caused by civil war, irrational economic policies, deliberate retribution or natural disasters. In addition, the number of people affected by famine has fallen compared with the late 19th century --not just as a percentage of the world's population but in absolute numbers.

" He has a point when he says that natural disasters, wars and poor economic policies are the causes of most famines. Maybe he forgot to leave out 'acts of God.' I don't know what percentage of famines are caused by each of the factors he listed. Some of course are caused by drought, but this would be a natural disaster.

"In the last century it was estimated that 70 million people died from famine. Some of these were natural disasters, by that I mean lack of water, freezing or too much heat-- such as in Bangladesh, Russia and the Sahel drought in Africa that killed 1 million people. There is no question that wars caused famines in many cases. But whatever the cause, the people are still dead. So famines do cause deaths when there are more people than there is food to feed them."

"He went on to say that food is abundant. Since 1948, according to the U.N. Food and Agriculture Organization and the U.S. Department of Agriculture, annual world food production has outpaced the increase in population by about 1 percent. Today, per capita production and per-acre yields are at all-time highs. Prices of agricultural products have been falling for more than 100 years. The average inflation-adjusted price of those products, indexed to wages, fell by more than 74% between 1950 and 1990. While Lester Brown of the Worldwatch Institute and the noted butterfly expert Paul Ehrlich predicted higher food prices and increasing scarcity, food is becoming cheaper and more plentiful. Anyway that's what he said. What is your answer to that Wreck?"

"There are famines today that are not even classed as famines because they are not so different from many countries' normal states of malnutrition. A recent situation in Malawi is such a situation, where many called it a famine. Let me give you some thoughts based on a book I read by Cormac Ó Gráda (30) First, he wrote that we need to define what a famine is. An accepted definition is that it is having one death per 10,000 people per day. A severe famine is twice that number. But some scholars would include a broader definition which would include endemic malnutrition. If we were to use that definition we have many famines across the world today. We can look at your informant's use of the term 'famine' without defining it is a semantic problem. Anyway most famines through history have been the result of poor harvests.

"While it is partially true that the worst 20th century famines were related to wars and revolutions, like those perpetrated by Mao and Stalin--that was not the whole story. In fact as far back as 2500 years ago there are records of Jewish and Roman famines related to war. But poor harvests like those in Niger and Southern Africa in the early part of this century were due primarily to crop failure. The Bengal famine of 1943–44, which killed well over two million, seems to have been a result of several possible causes, none directly attributable to war. A cyclone hit the area destroying many rice fields. There seems to have been an influx of a plant disease that may have destroyed many of the crops. There was also a large export of rice to British troops in other parts of the world. The North Korean famine of the 1990s has been estimated to have killed from a quarter million to over 3 million people. It was caused by a number of floods and by the fact that the Soviet Union could no longer supplement the food needs of North Korea. Then there was the drought and the economic incompetence of the

Zimbabwean government in 2002 that resulted in another major famine.

"Famines in the past have been related to crop failures, violent actions, and economic factors like when a controlling country takes the food produced in one country away from the farmers and sells it to the highest bidders. But in any case famines are due to a lack of food in an area because of natural or social causes. The point is people are still starving, there wasn't enough food produced to feed them--too many people for the food available.

"Violent social actions, like wars, may not necessarily be the cause of the famine, but they can increase the negative effects from a very poor harvest. This happened in the Soviet Union in 1932 and 33 and in China from 1959 to 1961. Just as ancient Egyptian famines were usually the result of the slower flow of the Nile, famines in the Indian subculture are often related to light monsoons. Throughout history droughts have generally been related to poor rainfall or too low river flows. Sometimes pests, like locusts or grasshoppers, are the cause. In temperate zones, cold and rain are more likely to be the problem

"In the late 1800s El Niño conditions in the Pacific led to a great deal of rainfall in Southeast Asia and Australasia, when the low pressure area shifted again it caused droughts in these areas. Even volcanic eruptions can cause growing problems for the countries affected by the clouds of ashes. And of course when armies burn the crops or salt the fields, or politicians implement poor economic plans, famine can be made more of a possibility. But the major cause is generally weather. So Ray, the protestations of the spokesman you are quoting are flawed. There may be contributing causes that increase the effects of a famine, but weather and pestilence are generally the fundamental causes. The point is that there were too many people for the food available.

"You said he was writing in 1993. So more than a few years have passed us by since then. You remember in 2008 there was a huge global food crisis. World prices for food nearly doubled in the previous two years. The poor, who usually spend 50 to 70% of their incomes on food, were hit extremely hard. There were food riots in 15 countries from Brazil to Bangladesh.

"In 2010 the United Nations' Food and Agricultural Organization, in its report on the Agricultural Outlook for 2010-2019, predicted that there will be still higher farm prices in the future. You can certainly understand this. With oil so important in agriculture and with its price reaching all-time highs, with fresh water being reduced, and with less arable land to grow food on, along with the growth in population, food prices obviously will continue to go higher. If you don't grow your own food you are going to have problems feeding yourself."

"The fellow I have been talking about criticized those who say that there are not enough fish in the ocean. People just say that there are fewer fish so they can raise the price of fish in the stores. They never consider things such as the fact that people are eating more meat and fish."

"None of those reasons disprove a lack of fish. I remember an old friend of mine Doctor Jed Gardner who retired from UCLA to a boat and sailed the world for years. He told me that in the earlier days he could drop a line and catch a tuna or a mahi-mahi within an hour, but by the turn of this century he said he could go all day without a nibble. Of course I realize that this illustration is logically fallacious because a single illustration doesn't prove the general application of the idea. But the reports of the fishing industry and various scientific agencies indicate that the ocean is definitely fished out in many areas.

" The UN Food and Agriculture Organization publishes a biannual status of the state of the world's fisheries and aquaculture.(31) In 2006 it was found that 52% of fish stocks are fully exploited, 20% were moderately exploited, 17% were over-exploited, 7% were depleted, and only 1% were recovering from having been depleted. It was also found that nearly 80% of the world's fisheries are fully or overtly exploited. And worldwide about 90% of the stocks of large predatory fish are already gone. The report goes on to say that we are not only losing species, but whole ecosystems. As an example in Newfoundland in 1992, there were no cod and the fishing industry came to a complete stop."

"I would agree with you on that one Wreck. But he didn't mention the extensive fish farming around the world that is supplying many of the needs of those who eat our finned friends. But then he went on to say something I do agree with, that farm lobbies influence governments to increase subsidies so that farm prices can be more profitable."

"I'd agree with that, too. But that just affects the prices in the more developed countries. It certainly doesn't affect subsistence farmers in adverse weather."

-"The spokesman for the Freedom Group said that you people who are predicting catastrophe for the years ahead are forgetting that the world is becoming a better place, more babies survive, people are living longer, and more people are surviving into old age. We should be celebrating this, not commiserating with these facts. Additionally, the replacement rate of 2.2 is being challenged. Many developed countries are below the level and the more fertile populations are reducing their fertility rates."

"Doesn't he see that these facts are part of the reasons for the world population problem. More people surviving their births and more people living to old age are challenging the earth's ability to provide for them. Does he offer any solutions to global warming, to the famines that are existing today, to the reduction in freshwater, to the problems of waste reduction, to the problems of natural resource depletion, or any of the other factors we have mentioned?

"Then we have talked about 2.2 or 2.1 necessary fertility rate as being outdated. It may have been predictive in the 1930s but it is far too high today with our longer lifespans.

"But let's get back on track. One study I read looked at the average fertility rate in a country and combined that with the average lifespan of a woman, then figuring how many years it would be before her female lineage ran out, so the lineage would produce no more babies. It concluded that for every baby born to a woman in the US it was like adding an additional 470 years to that woman with her present day pollution level-- including her car driving, energy use, and other polluting factors. In comparison to this every child born in China would be like adding 341 years to life of its mother. In India it was like adding 161 years per child to the life of the mother. In Japan it was 211 years and in Nigeria 136.

"When we look at birthrates of over seven per woman in Afghanistan, Niger and some other countries and birthrates in the 5 to 6 level for women in most of sub-Saharan Africa and in Palestine we can see some problems. Guatemala, Iraq and the remaining African countries are all over four babies per woman. Most of the Pacific Island nations are just under four babies per woman. Most of the Mideast countries are over three. India is now down to 2.8. The world as a whole is over 2.5, so we are well over the replacement rate of 2 to 2.2. In fact 130 of the 200 plus countries in the United Nations list were over two babies per woman. Only Hong Kong and Macau were under one child per female.(33) But maybe we need to follow Hong Kong to make a significant reduction in the world's overpopulation.

"His major points related to the reduction of freedom that population control might have--such as forced contraception, abortion or financial penalties for having more children than the government allows. He quoted the University of California professor who said that 'wealthier is healthier' and pointed to the increased wealth in the Western world."

"Well he did say that in 1993 and we're a number of years past that. He wasn't aware of the financial problems that the Western world faced in its recession at the end of the first decade of this century. People did get poorer. Governments increased their national debts and many people and some governments faced bankruptcy. So with hindsight being 20/20 we see that his predictions for the future were faulty. When he said that the increasing life expectancy in the developing world can therefore not be considered a sign of poverty He may have been right. But if we were to put this in the form of a syllogism and look at it logically, we would have: Wealthier is healthier. The Western world is healthier. So the Western world is wealthier. Do you see the fallacies here?

"Well first we have this semantic problems of defining wealth and health. Then we have the inductive problem of determining whether 'wealthier' is actually 'healthier.' Health was defined as living longer and having more babies survive. There are certainly many other factors that could go into a definition of 'healthier.' We could look at the level of diseases that people have, such as heart disease and cancer. We could look at the communicable diseases they might have, like HIV. We could look at the mental health of the people, such as how many are depressed or neurotic, how many are alcoholics or drug users. Then we could look at the deduction to see if the argument is valid. To restate the terms of the syllogism we would say 'Some wealthier societies are some of the healthier societies. The next term would be 'all of the Western world is some of the healthier societies.' Would we include Costa Rica as a Western country since its people live longer than those in US? Would we include Vietnam or Oman since their people live longer than those in Poland or the Czech Republic? So here 'Western world' obviously means 'some.' So that major deductive fallacy of the undifferentiated middle term is present because 'healthier' in both of the terms only refers to 'some' and not 'all' of the healthy people are healthy societies. So there are a good many logical fallacies in his primary statement.
(32)

"Then he said that while the world's population grew six-fold GDP rose eighty-fold. So the lengthening life expectancy in the developing world is evidence that population growth cannot be increasing poverty. He made the point that in our own century we have seen a replay of the Industrial Revolution. After World War II the population of Hong Kong grew more quickly than that of 19th century England or 20th century India -- at the same time that the resource-poor island colony was growing rich. The experiences of Japan, South Korea and Singapore reinforce the point."

"But South Korea imports 70% of its food, Japan 60% and Singapore 90%. It seems to me that those who argue against the idea that the world is overpopulated are libertarian. The libertarians seem to hold the idea of liberty over the necessity for survival. I certainly believe that survival is our basic human need and human right. If you're going to choose which route would you take?"

"And there are so many religious people who, for some reason, want an unlimited number of people on the planet. And of course God will provide for them just as he has done in Darfur, Bangladesh, Haiti and the ghettos and barrios of many countries. Not long ago I saw a statement on a website that said that the state of Montana could handle all the people of the world and each would have a square kilometer for himself. The truth is that with a land area of 145,552 square miles, 376,980 square kilometers, each of the people would have 0.000057 of a square kilometer. That's 68 square yards or 57 square meters or 6 thousandths of a hectare. And according to experts at Cornell University we need about 800 times that much arable land per person. But in Montana there isn't really that much arable land. About 40% is water, rivers and lakes, and mountains. So the illustration given becomes even more ridiculous. That is so often true of people trying to counter an intelligent argument by making up their own statistics."

"How many people will the Earth hold? With 510 million square kilometers of land and sea if we give every person one square meter we could stack 70,000 times more people on the Earth. If we look at just at the land, with 149 million square kilometers, we could have 20,000 times the number of people we have now. But since many might object to living on the polar ice, the world's deserts or the rocky mountains of the world we should just use the arable land. There are 31 million square kilometers of arable land, so if we settled the people only on the arable land and gave them each one square meter we could have four thousand times the number of people we have now, That would be about 28 trillion people."

"With each person having about 10 square feet, or one square meter, for living, raising his food, parking his car, and for living and sleeping, there wouldn't be any room for roads, factories, grocery stores, hospitals, doctors' offices, pharmacies or anything else.

"Right now if we give everyone about a half an acre instead of a square meter we can handle about the number of people we have now.

"But I'm not sure that more growth is really possible in many parts of the planet. Nature seems to have placed limits on its resources. When there are too many lemmings they jump off a cliff. When old redwoods reach three or four hundred feet they stop growing. In our human realm, when people or governments borrow too much, their economies falter and recession or depression sets in. So it seems that in both the natural and social areas that affect human life, too much of something can crash the system."

"I am thinking of some other ridiculous growth factors. In ancient days some Chinese let their fingernails grow to a foot or two. Naturally they couldn't do anything for fear of breaking their overgrown fingernails. It seems that excess population growth develops similar problems. Remember in 2010 when there was that huge earthquake in Haiti and nearly 200,000 died? The island could not support its population. There was inadequate arable land. Incompetent builders working with inferior building codes and building materials had erected buildings that could not withstand a large earthquake. With a higher standard of living and greater expectations for the people, California's building codes and building materials were designed to handle earthquakes much more effectively. So it's just not the number of people but the standard of living that they might enjoy that we might be concerned with. After all, Haiti has the potential to be an island paradise."

"You may remember that south of Stanford in San Jose there is the Winchester House where the woman who owned it continued to build until she died. She thought that if shecontinued building she wouldn't die. There were stairs going nowhere, rooms with no purpose, and no design. It was just growth for growth's sake. Her neurosis may not have been harmful to the world, but the societal psychosis of those who propose the same unthought-out design for an overpopulated society are building a mausoleum for humanity. The uncontrolled growth of population is having the same effect on developing a healthy human society that an uncontrolled cancer has on developing a healthy human body.

"So Wreck, you obviously have to change most people's opinions. But which road will you take? Economics can scare some Westerners into smaller families. It already has, and has for years. When both partners in a relationship are happy working and delighted to use their increased income for financial frivolities like fancy cars, more lavish homes and interesting vacations—you have an effective economic incentive. But in societies where a man's wealth and power are measured by the size of his family, not by the size of his house, you will have a lot of educating to do."

WHAT IS A MAXIMUM POPULATION FOR THE WORLD?

"People have been proposing maximum population for the Earth for 250 years. The first one that I know of was Anthony Leeuwenhoek, the father of the microscope, who thought the earth could hold 13 1/2 billion people. That was in 1679. Since that time a number of people have guessed from a half a billion to a trillion people could inhabit of our planet. Some of these have merely been guesses based on the landmass of the earth. More recently guesses have been made based on the potential amount of arable land, the amount of water available, and the living standard that those people might enjoy.

"I saw an interesting estimation of how many people the world could hold depending on their economic level. If we lived at the level of the average Indian, the world might be able to support 18 1/2 billion people. If we live at the level of Ethiopia, we could support half that many. If we lived at the level of South Korea we could support a little over 4 billion people. If we lived at the level of Canada we could support about 1.9 billion. And if we all lived at the level of the United States we could support just under 1 1/2 billion people.(34) I don't know how true it is, but the point is that not everyone can live at an advanced economic level if we have more people than the natural resources can support.

"Of course if we only allotted one square foot per person of all land in the world, including the non-arable land, we could fit in 160 quadrillion people, that's 160 followed by fifteen zeros.

WHERE IS THE MONEY FOR REDUCING OVERPOPULATION?

"A study from the London School of Economics concluded that if the money spent for climate change was spent for condoms we would save five times as much money as that spent on low carbon emission technology. The study was based on the numbers of women who want family planning but are not using it for one reason or another. So money made available to those who want contraception was considered to be able to reduce the births by 72% among the 200 million women who wanted contraception. If this were done half a billion fewer babies would be born by 2050, so the population in that year would only be about 8.6 billion.

"It further laid out the relative costs for this program. To reduce a ton of carbon dioxide would cost $7 using condoms, $24 using wind power, $51 using solar power, about $70 using coal plants with carbon capture, $92 for hybrid vehicles and $131 for electric vehicles.

THE CARBON FOOTPRINT OF EVERY NEW BABY

"Researchers Murtaugh and Schlax, of Oregon State University, found that for each child a woman has in the U.S. it adds 9,441 metric tons of carbon dioxide to her 'carbon legacy.' This is equivalent to the emissions from burning 972,160 gallons of gasoline.(35) Consequently a country that is concerned with planetary survival might well think of limiting births.

"A problem is that it is usually the predominantly white countries that are telling the predominantly darker skinned countries, where the birthrates are quite high, to reduce their birthrates. This is often seen as genocide. But we have to realize that the carbon footprint of a child born in El Salvador or Bangladesh is much less than that of one born in the US or Western Europe. But then we could also look at the expected happiness of a child born in a Third World country versus a child born in a developed country.

BUSINESS INTERESTS AND THE PROPAGANDA OF SKEPTICISM

"Pro-business media outlets, like the Wall Street Journal or the Rupert Murdoch media, naturally take a pro-business rather than a pro-planet position. They usually say that technology will save us. But there is a huge cost to that technology that will give us pollution free energy, desalinated salt water, and new arable land from mountains and deserts. And they never mention how all this increased technology will increase the number of jobs available for all the people, when robots and computers will be doing so much of the work. And of course they never mention what a maximum or optimal planetary population would be.

"There is always the clash between the individual self-centered desires, often influenced by tradition and religion, and the society desires--society meaning the world society, the national society, the business society, and so forth. We will never be able to satisfy everyone. The major questions are whether we should be concerned about the annihilation of the people on the planet or the decreasing comfort level of its inhabitants. Many societies are concerned with the cost of supporting their citizens economically, politically, and into their old age. At this point in time there is not enough money in any society to do all these things.

"Should parents be responsible for all of the costs of the children that they bring into the world? This might include their carbon footprint, their health and medical bills, their education expenses, and even their retirement costs? We might see some of these ideas in a society when we visit the United Colonies on our trip. The have instituted some requirements for parents to pay for their children.

CONFRONTING SKEPTICS ON FOOD SHORTAGES

"Let's move on. The skeptics who don't believe there are food shortages for our rapidly growing population usually point to an idea that there is plenty of food but it's a transportation problem to deliver it. They may point to the Green Revolution and to genetically modified seeds that can increase production and reduce pestilence. But it's not that simple. Arable land is decreasing, the amount of land per person is decreasing, and the amount of water available is decreasing, the cost of gasoline is increasing for those who use machines in their farming. This all results in increased costs for food.

"Since 1960 global food production has increased 25% while world population doubled. African food production decreased 10% while its population increased by 40% in spite of the wars and genocide.

"Rising food prices result from several factors. Increasingly, the rich people don't merely rely on staples such as wheat and corn, they want beef, tomatoes, and wine. The beef is usually fed corn. Some corn is used in biofuels. I've heard that a quarter of all grain crops find their way into the gas tank. Meanwhile, the poor African living on fifty cents to $2 a day can't buy staples. The increasing cost of water for irrigation, the increased costs of supplies such as fertilizers and pesticides, and the increased cost of oil all contribute to the eventual cost of food."(35a)

"About half the world's land is now grazed by cattle and sheep, but over a third of the grain produced in the world is fed to livestock. In the US, of its 312 million tons of grain produced in a year, 135 million tons are fed to livestock. This would be enough to feed 400 million vegetarians. But you can understand that with our self-centered values and our tastes for beef, lamb and chicken-- our grains go to animals, not Africans.

"Twenty years ago, in a two-year period, the prices for wheat, rice and corn tripled. I'm glad that I had money invested in corn futures. I made a bundle. It was only with the great recession of 2009 that food prices reduced temporarily. In the past, price surges were caused by unusual heat waves or a lack of rain, but those temporary occurrences are now being replaced by long-term factors such as global warming, aquifer reductions, reduced arable land, the increased cost of fertilizer and fuel to run the farm equipment, and of course the major problem is that there are more mouths to feed, increasing by many millions each year."

"With the sea level rising, river deltas like the Mekong and Nile can be permanently under seawater. A rise of 1 to 2 meters is devastating to local farming. The Mekong Delta produces half of the rice in Vietnam, and Vietnam is the world's second largest rice exporter. A one meter rise in sea level would cover half of the rice growing area in Bangladesh, a country of 140 million people with the world's most dense population.

"The wheat and rice harvests of China and India would be directly affected. China is the world's leading wheat producer. India is second. The U.S. is only third. With rice, China and India totally dominate the world harvest. The projected melting of the Himalayan glaciers poses the most massive threat to food security the world has ever faced.

"At the end of the last century the number of hungry people in world was reducing. It leveled out at about 825 million. Ten years into this century it had already topped a billion. When we look at previous civilizations such as the Sumerians and the Mayans we see that it was food shortages that destroyed them. Will food shortages destroy all or part of today's world society?

"In the 1960s most countries were self-sufficient in food. Today only a few are. Canada and the US are usually among the few food exporters. The Green Revolution increased grain production, which more than doubled. But the Green Revolution put a strain on the ecology by increasing soil erosion, polluting groundwater and surface water with pesticides, which has caused some health problems. Eight percent less land is now being used for grain production. In Africa per capita grain production has gone down about 1% a year.

Yet with the population doubling in order to feed the world and increase the level of nutrition for the malnourished it is estimated that we need a tripling of agricultural production. But nearly all of the world's arable land that has the potential for agriculture is already in use. The remaining land is too steep, too cold, too wet or too dry for agricultural use. What increase there has been in arable land has been because of deforestation.

"Soil erosion by wind and water is a major problem in terms of increasing agricultural production. It takes about 500 years to replace one inch of topsoil. So topsoil is being lost more than 100 times faster than it is being formed. Worldwide, soil erosion over the last 40 years has caused farmers to abandon over 430 million hectares, over a billion acres. Much of this is the result of building on arable land.

"In spite of the fact that arable land is disappearing, the use of effective fertilizers and genetically enhanced seeds have increased the average yield per hectare so that food production has not reduced as much as might be expected from the loss of arable land. But this increase in production cannot be expected to make up for the loss of land, and by 2050 we expect very severe problems in terms of food production for the world's population."

WHAT CAN WE DO?

"But there is some hope. Science is working to reduce the negative impacts on our arable land and to increase our crop yields. By increasing the use of pesticides and fertilizers we can increase crop yields in some areas, but the problems we just talked about will increase. Animals can graze on grass and shrubs and don't have to be fed grains, although the grains certainly make them fatter and juicier.

"If new plant varieties can be developed that will use nitrogen from the air for fertilizer and resist plant and pest damage, it would certainly help the situation. Pests destroy about a third of the average crops produced in the world. Pesticides that could break down into harmless substances before poisoning the land or water would be an advantage. Better irrigation would be a positive, but with decreasing freshwater available the question is where to find it.

OTHER CONSIDERATIONS

"Global warming requires that we reduce fossil fuel use and stop deforestation. Both of these seem to be highly unlikely if we are to increase food supplies. About a half a hectare, or an acre and a quarter, is about what is needed to feed one person eating a combination vegetable and animal diet. We are now at less than half that amount of land per person. And with the population increasing at about 2% a year, food production needs to increase at over 3% per year. During the Green Revolution grain production was increasing at almost 3% a year, but that level has long since reduced. However some countries in Asia and Latin America are increasing their annual grain yields.

"In 25 years, by 2050, the land used for grain production will have been reduced from 718 million hectares in 1982 to 620 million. With the expected increase in population it will be about six hundredths of a hectare, about 700 square meters per person—less than 6 people per acre of arable land. So if we need one and a quarter acres now, we will have one sixth of an acre in 2050—you can understand the problem. On the somewhat positive side, there are estimates that we will have 1000 square meters per person—four people per acre.(35b) Irrigated land will yield up to 100 bushels of wheat per acre per year, about 250 per hectare, and non-irrigated land about 1/3 to 1/2 that much. That would be about 44 loaves of bread per person from irrigated acres and 15 to 20 from non-irrigated acres per person per year. Higher income Americans eat about a fifth of a loaf per day, poor people eat much more. So for a rich American his share of bread would last him almost 8 months. But if you were a poor person with irrigated land it would last you about four months, but if you were a poor person with non-irrigated land the bread would last you only about two months.

"The world seems to be at its limit in terms of food production capacity using only farmland. It is a combination of too many people, not enough water, increased costs of fertilizers, and reducing the amount of arable land. To remedy these problems would require huge capital expenses. Governments don't seem ready to make such commitments yet, and with the increasing national debts of nearly every country it is likely that they will not make such investments.(36) Vertical farming has been thought of but it is generally dismissed as being impractical. The plans for hydroponic farms in tall buildings would require a great deal of experience to build the building. Mirrors might be used to direct sunlight into the plant growing rooms. However human or robotic power would still be needed to plant and harvest the food.

CONFRONTING THE SKEPTICS ON WATER SHORTAGES

"I guess I can expect some people to be skeptical about the shortages of fresh water we are facing even if our population doesn't increase."

"As long as you're going to approach your quest with reason, you'd better be prepared for any skeptics, I guess I mean 'many' skeptics. Here is one tidbit. Did you know that 15% of India's grain harvest is produced by pumping groundwater. Those wells are rapidly going dry. 130 million Chinese are facing the same problem of the depletion of groundwater. So are Pakistan, Iran, Yemen and many other countries.

"You know that 70% of our Earth's surface is water, but only 3% is freshwater, and only 1% is readily available in streams, lakes, aquifers, and rivers. The rest of freshwater is in ice. And not all of the fresh water is clean. In the more primitive areas of the world where people live by rivers, those at the source may get clean water but then they excrete into the water so that the next town or village will be drinking somewhat dirty water. And so forth all the way down the river to the mouth. In an advanced society that drinking water would be treated before it is drunk, and the sewage would be purified before it was sent down the river to the next town.

"Water is not dispersed equally across the globe. A country like Norway with its small population, its long snowy winter, its rainy summers, and its many mountains and rivers, has no problem. But countries in the Mideast, like Israel or Saudi Arabia, get little rainfall so have major problems in providing water for their populations. It has been estimated that it takes a minimum of 12 gallons of water to provide for the drinking needs, the food production, and the sanitation needs of a person every day. The average American uses about 160 gallons daily.

"If we remember Maslow's priority of needs, remember that water is second only to the air we breathe in our human physiological priorities. So if we can't provide water for everyone we are certainly going to have trouble, and I mean trouble on an international scale.

DRINKING WATER

"When governments have the money they can treat the sewage and reuse the water for farming. This is a so-called 'gray' water. Some areas, like Los Angeles, are even working on projects to make sewage water drinkable. Those living near salt water can desalinize it, but it is very expensive. Southern Spain and the Canary Islands, because of their tourist trade, can profitably desalinize water and pass the costs to the tourists."

IRRIGATION

"Water is even a more of a limiting factor than the loss of the land. As an illustration, to produce 7000 kilograms of corn in a hectare it would take a meter of water in the form of rain falling at the proper time on that hectare during the growing season. This is a highly unlikely possibility. That of course is why we use irrigation. But only about 16% of cropland is irrigated. And that irrigated land yields over twice as much food per acre as the non-irrigated land. But irrigation takes huge amounts of water, in fact about 70% of the water that we humans use is used in irrigation. It takes 1400 liters of water to produce just one kilogram of corn. It takes more than twice that much to produce a kilogram of rice.

"You know Wreck that when you estimate water use there are a huge number of variables to consider. For example if you're talking about growing grains, it takes more water to grow grain in a warm climate where there is a great deal of evaporatra or where there is a lot of runoff because of the hardness of the soil. But at least we have some idea of the modern water needed to produce food or manufactured goods. Let me check it on my iPhone now. Here are some estimates from this web page. It says it takes about 520 gallons of water to manufacture a car tire and 62,000 gallons of water to manufacture a ton of steel. Here's something else on food. It says that it takes about 16,000 liters of water to produce a kilogram of beef, that's about 2000 gallons of water for pound of meat. And here's an interesting one. It says that takes 120 gallons of water to manufacture one egg. Can you believe that it takes over 6500 gallons of water to produce the cotton needed for one tee shirt?"

"Interesting! As you might imagine with the increase in population, the per capita amount of irrigated land is continually being reduced. Another problem is that irrigated land, when not using pure rainwater, uses groundwater and other water that has picked up salts. The salts then salinize the soil and, in effect, poison it. This is particularly true in Australia, the US, Mexico, Egypt, Pakistan and India. This salinization results in the loss of about 1% of the world's farmland annually. Traditionally this has been made up by increasing the amount of land that is irrigated. So today in 2025 we have lost about 25% of the farmland we had at the turn-of-the-century. And in 25 more years we will have lost another 25%. You can understand how these losses are very difficult to make up, especially when we are trying to feed more people every year with less land.

"Then as you can surmise, the runoff of the irrigating water which has been poisoned by pesticides and fertilizers negatively affects the streams and rivers below the irrigated land."

GLACIER MELT

"We have already talked about the glaciers of the Himalayas that feed the headwaters of the Ganges, Mekong, Indus, Yangtse and Brahmaputra rivers. They supply at least some of the water for half of the world's population. According to the Water Management Institute, most of Southeast Asia already has a shortage of water. In five years, in 2030, India will have only half of the water that it needs to sustain its population at the level it had in 2010. In fact the world will have 40% less water than it needs in 2030.

LOSS OF WATER TABLES

"Africa and several countries in the Middle East, especially Israel and Jordan, as well as other countries, are depleting fossil groundwater resources. China has severe agricultural problems. In China, ground water levels are falling as much as a meter a year in the major wheat and corn growing regions of the north China Plain. Other areas in China report groundwater levels dropping at four times that rate. And in parts of India they are falling at 2 1/2 to 3 meters a year.

"In 2008 Saudi Arabia, which had been self-sufficient in raising wheat for over 20 years, announced that the aquifer it had used for its irrigation was largely depleted. They saw that as it depleted their wheat production was reduced by 12% per year until 2016 when they could no longer produce grain. They had to increase their wheat imports yearly to feed their 30 million population, a population the same size as Canada's. The Saudis, because of their nonexistent rainfall, must irrigate any crops they grow. And countries like China and India, even with a good amount of rainfall, still require water for irrigation and that water is disappearing too. California's Central Valley has the problem now. Even though the state reduced the amount of water for farmers, many communities still don't have water to drink. Texas is having problems too.

DROUGHTS

"Droughts are a fact of the nature of climate. There are wet years and dry years. When you have desert areas such as in the southwest United States, from California to Texas, the effects of a lack of rain are greatly magnified when the population increases. A drought in southern California or Arizona in 1850 when there were a few hundred thousand people could be managed more readily than they can today with their multi-millions of people. The California drought in the early part of this century dropped the water reserves to under a year in 2015 and homes in Southern California had water bills of over a thousand dollars a month. Studies at Columbia University have indicated this clearly. And you can guess that the global warming will undoubtedly increase the droughts in some parts of the world.

WATER DISPUTES AND WATER WARS

"In 1995, World Bank Vice President Ismail Serageldin said, 'the wars of the next century will be fought over water.' The first war fought over water was 4,500 years ago in Mesopotamia. More recently the genocidal conflict in Darfur early in this century that killed as many as 400,000 Africans, started, in part, over access to a diminishing water supply. Darfur started as a local conflict but eventually included a whole region. Because water supplies are not usually enclosed entirely within one country, water disputes can arise. If the country takes too much of the water upriver, the people downriver will probably suffer. There are many parts of the world where water rights are already a problem.

"Even in the United States there have been problems between Alabama, Florida and Georgia over a dwindling supply of water. Arizona and California have had problems over the distribution of water from the Colorado River. As Arizona's population has increased it has needed to call on a greater percentage of the river water that was originally allocated to it. Even within California, where the high rainfall in the north usually has plenty of water, the desert of Southern California does not have enough. The Southern Californians want to share the Northern Californian watery wealth, but their northern brothers are not quite ready 'to share and share alike'"

"That's right Con, we will probably have to cut back on our traditionally luxurious habits. You can imagine that with the increasing population, with our decreasing water and with our increasing temperatures, the poorer starving and dehydrating people of the world might be likely terrorist converts against the richer well-watered countries. If there are such things as human rights, as the United Nations would like us to believe, access to water would have to be extremely high on that list. We think of safety as being high on the UN's list of human rights, but life's requirements of air, water, and food must be at least as high as safety in the priority of basic rights."

"Commander, I think your global education program must emphasize the growing need for water, based not only on population increases, but also the needs of technology, and of course, the needs for agriculture to supply food to the growing population. Water may be our most important economic need and it is certainly our most important natural resource. And it doesn't increase as population increases—it is reducing. By that I mean that as warming increases the melting of the polar ice caps, that freshwater enters the ocean and becomes salty. So our warming is actually reducing potential freshwater available to humans.

"One obvious solution is to build dams. But the dams cover a good bit of arable land. They also lose much of the water they hold to evaporation. Another problem is that there are natural salts in fresh water and the salts can accumulate in the lakes behind the dam. Then when that water is used for irrigation the salts can poison the farmland. We have already mentioned some of those problems of salinization."

"An illustration of the problem of reducing water supplies can be seen in the US where the town of Orme in Tennessee ran out of water in 2007. But the neighboring town of New Hope, Alabama allowed the people of Orme to bring in trucks to take back water to fill the town's water tank. Then they allowed a two-mile long pipe to bring Orme water from New Hope. So cooperation sometimes eliminates possible conflicts.

"To help to solve the water problem, more efficient uses of water are possible. About 70% of all water used by humans is used in agriculture and about 40% of that is lost through evaporation and inefficient irrigation methods. If the more modern drip-irrigation technique is used, about 95% of the water would be used efficiently. Another way to save water is to plant crops that are genetically modified to grow with little or no water. Desalinization, which we already mentioned, is expensive but the costs are coming down. My experience though is that they use so much chlorine to purify it that it tastes terrible. Of course another method is to just make water more expensive so that people will conserve more. But then the poor would be hurt the most.

"I have heard a new term, 'water footprint.' As in the 'carbon footprint,' America leads the way, or should I say hogs the way. The average American uses about 2,500 cubic meters of water a year. That's enough to fill an Olympic size pool. I am talking here about water used for personal use, like bathing, and water used to irrigate the food we eat and water used in the production of things we use. The world average water usage is about half that of an American. And the average Chinese uses less than a third of what an American uses.

POLLUTED WATER

"There are many types of polluted water. It can be polluted by sewage, by pesticides, by naturally occurring toxins such as arsenic, and by other factors. In Bangladesh, for example, about half of its 150 million people have drunk tainted water, much of it with

arsenic. Arsenic can cause a number of diseases such as cancers, liver problems, and heart disease. In a study funded by the US National Institutes of Health, 1 in 5 deaths during the 10 years of the study were attributable to arsenic poisoning. But the physical health problems are only part of the picture, people who are known to be drinking arsenic tainted water are often found to be seen in a lower social status than they would normally occupy. This then can affect their choice of marriage mates and other socially determined factors in the lifestyle."

CONFRONTING THE SKEPTICS ON LICENSING PARENTS

"Well we have covered water problems now let's look at the problem that will obviously be your greatest hurdle commander. When you suggest licensing parents in order to improve the life of the children born, and at the same time possibly reduce population, you are fighting a far larger windmill than Don Quixote ever imagined. You know that you will be fighting the conservative religions as well as the conservative traditions that have been with us as long as we have been an 'us'-- whether we look at Adam and Eve, the first Neanderthals, or the earlier hominids--having babies was the way of life. And certainly it had its uses. It provided young hands to aid the family's survival. Of course then there wasn't the option of contraception or abortion. But even if there had been I doubt that it would have been used. But then we know that often in primitive societies infanticide has been, and is, used to cull the unneeded infants.

"Let's first look at the problems and then we might have a better way to approach the skeptics."

TEEN BIRTHS

"In our country, Wreck, you might look at trying to reduce teen births. We have a an extremely high rate of teenage pregnancies. Many seem to be accidental but some are planned among the unmarried. After all what is more adult than for a girl than to be a mother and what is more adult than for a boy than to be a father. I'm facetious, of course, but teenagers so often want what they see as the accouterments of adulthood. Smoking, drinking, impregnating or being impregnated certainly rank right up there with what adults can do.

"Look at the number of teenage births in the West. A few years ago there were 31 births per 1,000 British girls aged between 15 and 19. In the US the figure was 52 per 1,000 births. It then began reducing and last I heard it was half that, about 26 per 1000; This was the highest rate in the developed world. This is in stark contrast to Korea's rate of three per thousand, Japan's rate of four per thousand, and China, Switzerland and the Netherlands with five per thousand. There were countries with even higher rates than US, with Mexico at 64, South Africa at 66 and Nigeria at 233. Of course in Niger nearly 90% of girls are married by the time they are 18, and over half have given birth by that time. But you can understand that a child growing up in Niger does not need all the social and economic tools that child growing up in a western country needs. So perhaps Commander, your message needs to be different depending on the economic level of the people you are attempting to educate."

"But an equally alarming fact for us Americans is that the states with the highest number of impoverished people had the highest number of teenage births. New Mexico, Texas, and Mississippi all had over 75 births for every thousand teenage girls. California had 59. On the other hand states with higher incomes and those that had the lowest percentage of people living in poverty had the lowest numbers of teenage births. New Hampshire with 28 births per thousand was second in per capita income.

"Sexual codes have become more relaxed without corresponding changes to prepare teenagers to cope with the new freedoms. In Europe it seems that the young are much better informed about sex. They not only develop healthier attitudes towards it but they also are much more likely to use contraceptives to prevent births. And if that fails, abortion is generally a possibility. But in our country teenagers are generally aware of how babies are made, but they tend to think that it won't happen to them. And often the sex seems to come as a surprise, so commonly people are not prepared with contraception."

"Probably! That's why I believe it should be should absolutely essential that teenagers use contraceptives, both to prevent pregnancy and to reduce the chances of picking up sexually transmitted diseases. In continental Europe, on the other hand, they seem to look at the body as good and sexual desires and activities as real, because of this their sex education from parents and schools is realistic. If sex is seen as a desirable activity and unwanted children are to be prevented, contraceptives and abortions become acceptable. The US and UK ideas of 'sex on a whim' is replaced on the continent with 'sex as a plan'.

"The age at which British youngsters lose their virginity has fallen from 20 for men and 21 for women 40 years ago, to 17 for both sexes today. In the US it is about 18 and for the Scandinavian countries about 16. The age of first sex has been steadily dropping while the age of first marriage has been steadily rising, or should I say persons living together, is occurring later. So there are longer periods of uncommitted relationships or immature relationships that need to be childless. The average age for entering committed relationships for Americans is about 28 and closer to 32 in the Scandinavian countries. So for half of their lives the Scandinavians have been sexually active. For Americans it's more like a third of their lives.

"Undoubtedly with the pressure from the movies and other media, earlier sex activities can be expected.

"As you know poverty increases the teenage birth rate. Whether it be an impoverished country or impoverished people in a richer country, it is true. For example in the UK 50% of all teenage pregnancies occur in the poorest 30% of the population. But only 14% of teenage pregnancies occur in the richest 30% of the population.

"Here is another consideration. At all levels of society domestic violence and family problems in childhood are more likely to be present among pregnant teenagers. It's also true of the fathers of the children of teenage mothers. This may indicate that what we talked of earlier, licensing parents to have children, might not only significantly reduce teenage pregnancy and the unwanted social cycle that it begins but could also reduce other negatives in our family lives. Studies also show that fathers who left their families in a child's early years had daughters who were more likely to become pregnant as teenagers. In fact when fathers left early in the lifecycle of the child in the United States it increased the chance of their daughters being pregnant in their teenage years by five times. In New Zealand it increased the rate by three times.

"It is obvious that having a child to care for will significantly affect a girl's chances of getting an education-- even finishing high school, and certainly of getting a college education at a young age. The realities are that they will have to get a low-level job to support themselves and their child. Less than a third of teenage mothers received child-support from the father. And money from the impoverished governments, as welfare, does not come close to meeting the monetary needs of the young mother.

Consequently teenage mothers are commonly required to work at low-level jobs to support their children. Another major consideration is that men are less likely to want to settle down with somebody who already has children that aren't theirs."

"When I was at Stanford I saw a study done on birthrates in Northern California. In Marin County, above San Francisco, there was a 5% poverty rate and the birth rate per thousand was five. In Tulare County, near Yosemite, with the non-Hispanic Caucasians the poverty rate was 18% and the birth rate of teenagers was 50 per thousand. In the same county for the Hispanics the poverty rate was 40% and the birth rate was 100 per thousand for teenagers.

"Did you know that teen pregnancy costs the United States over $7 billion annually. That could certainly be a reason to require licenses to have babies. Can you imagine the wails we would hear if abortions were required of all teenage girls who didn't have licenses? I wonder if the tax protesters would be 'for' or 'against' saving $7 billion if it required abortions."

"I didn't realize that. In my quest to reduce births, it's hard to know where to begin. In the underdeveloped farming countries the extra hands may be of value, but the extra babies are going to put a strain on the economic hopes for most poor people. Maybe we need to work on increasing education at the same time we are trying to reduce population.

If we look at the West, we can generally see that increased education results in higher economic achievement, more contentment with one's life, and a reduction in the fertility rates. Still we have too many unloved children, too much juvenile delinquency and to many people imprisoned because of their lack of social concern.

"Should I approach governments to increase their education offerings relative to reducing pregnancy? Should I approach them to reduce or eliminate financial help for unwed mothers? We certainly all feel sympathy for the children born, because it wasn't their fault. And yet it seems certain that the children of these unwed mothers are highly likely to continue to be financial drains on the society through their lack of educational achievement, their increased criminal behavior which strains the justice system, and their propensity to imitate their parents' lack of concern for parenthood.

"Poverty and lack of education are major reasons for teenage births. In the developed countries, marriage or committed relationships are often put off into the future because of education needs, a lack of money or a realization that maturity has not yet been achieved. Because of this it seems that 'play' is the order of the day. And it's unrealistic to expect teenagers to hold off sex until they're married when that marriage may not occur until the 30s or 40s. It was one thing to hold off sex until after marriage when you married at 20 to 25. It is quite another when you may never get married or may never be in a committed relationship. It seems that there are too many people trying to fit all teenagers into some sort of an idealized non-sexual society."

"Poverty is certainly a major factor in teenage births. It may be societal poverty which often includes teenage brides, such as in India, the Mideast, and much of Southeast Asia. This poverty is more likely to be continued when there is a lack of effective education. And a lack of education begets poverty. So we have a cycle, negative cycle, poorly educated people indulging in carnal pleasures, and adding to the world more impoverished and uneducated beings.

"At all levels of society, domestic violence and family problems in childhood are more likely to be present among pregnant teenagers. It's also is true of the fathers of the children of teenage mothers. This may indicate that what we talked of earlier, licensing parents to have children, might well significantly reduce teenage pregnancy and the unwanted social cycle that it begins.

COST OF A CHILD

"Wreck, you can certainly mention the cost of raising children. The greed of parents who want to spend their money on bigger cars or houses or vacations would perk up some ears. And the desire generated by people's drives for success, for financial or vocational power, or for meaningful jobs in research, teaching or civil service, have already slowed birth rates in developed countries.

"It may not help to show the actual cost of raising a child, but it wouldn't hurt.

"I know that the U.S. Department of Agriculture puts out reports periodically on the cost of having children and raising them to college age. The last I saw it was about $220,000 counting housing, food, child care, clothing, and the numerous other expenses relating to education and recreation.(37) In fact the Department has an interesting analysis depending on where you live and how many children you have. It can be accessed easily on the Internet.(37a) It is obvious that children born to poor people will not have the same advantages that these middle class children have.

"People just don't think of the dollars and cents involved."

CONFRONTING THE SKEPTICS ON PARENT LISCENSING

"Well, let me see who the opponents of any type of licensing might be. It is obvious that business wants more customers, so that they might be an enemy. The conservative religions, trying to increase their flocks while increasing their political clout, may be the major opposition. Of course there will be those who want more children for whatever selfish reasons they may have, like showing how fertile they are. Some governments will certainly fight the idea of limiting births because they need to keep up their tax intake and they need more soldiers.

"I think the key is the government. But in democratic governments the people have to be persuaded. So where do we begin?"

"You're right, Wreck, this will be your toughest challenge. Maybe you should just concentrate on trying to reduce the population. But I understand your concern that every child should have loving parents who will help the child to become its best self.

"Maybe if you concentrated on reducing teenage pregnancy you would have the blessings of the government and probably the blessings of the teenagers' parents. Probably a very strong education program in parenting education as well as sex education would help. I know you've seen those health education projects where the teacher assigns each child to care for an egg for a week. The students name the egg and may even make clothes for it. They have to provide for feeding the egg, and if for a period of time they can't take care of it they need to get a babysitter, I mean an egg-sitter. This lesson may help many to understand that there is more to caring for a child than just conceiving it.

"Maybe the media could be enlisted to show how difficult it is for teenagers to raise a child. Along with that they might show how a child reduces the dating desirability of the teenaged parent. In fact it tends to reduce the dating desirability of adults also. As you just mentioned, other things being equal, why would a man want to take responsibility for somebody else's child? So there is a huge social negative to being a single teenaged parent. For many, a child will reduce, and often eliminate one's chances for an effective education. This of course reduces the chance of getting the type of job that one would prefer. Then of course there is the cost of the child, which is much more than a government stipend would pay. Another factor could be that because so many unloved girls want a baby to love them, an education program should include the fact that babies can't love. The parent must be able to love the child so that eventually the child will be capable of loving. But of course these ideas assume that rationality can overcome the psychological needs for power that many teenagers believe will be satisfied if they become parents."

"You will have an impossible task trying to change the Catholic, Mormon and Muslim beliefs that God told us to procreate."

"But Father Ray, aren't you living in opposition to the command to procreate since you are celibate?"

"Lee, you know that my celibacy precludes the marriage duty to procreate. As St. Paul wrote to the Corinthians, 'it is best for a man not to touch a woman.' So we have Paul's ascetic admonition versus that for families, such as Adam and Eve. In many religions asceticism is practiced by those who are holiest."

"Okay Ray, so Godly people shouldn't have children but married people should. What about those who are neither Godly nor married? Should the unwed therefore not have children? If so, the religions shouldn't object to unmarried people either being required to have licenses or not being allowed to have children.'

-"Maybe not. But if unmarried people conceive a child, they should marry."

"Is that a Church law or just a personal opinion?"

"Just an opinion."

"So maybe I should first concentrate on the unmarried teenagers needing licenses. That would fall under the political rule of 'divide and conquer.' I would probably have fewer objections from those over 20 and those who are married."

"But what kind of license would you suggest?"

"The things we talked about before. It could be just age, like having to be 16 or 18 or 20. It could be that you have to have graduated from high school. It could be that you had to take a course in parenthood. I don't think initially it could be all that tough. Just some minimum qualifications that are easy to assess."

"I think you're right about starting with unmarried teenagers. You have to get your foot in the door. It's like when a government starts a sales tax they start with 1% this year, then as the years roll on they raise it as needed. So as a politician you start to change a program with the smallest group with the weakest voice. Once your idea is established and people are numbed a bit to the concept, you can go to the next level."

"I would think that the first place to start would be with women who don't want children and haven't the means for contraception. I think you want to start with the voluntary aspects before you move to any legal requirements.

"You are certainly going to have people bringing up the China policy of one child. They may bring up the fact that there were many more boys than girls, that they may need more babies to pay for the pensions of the older people. They may even criticize China for not being a real democracy.

"That's probably quite true. But I think I'd answer them this way. The one child policy was certainly better for the world than the previous ideas of having as many babies as you want. Certainly China's policy has been a major factor in their economic success. While the policy started in the late 1970s, the population kept rising until 2015 when it reached 1.4 billion, then it started to reduce. The population in 2010 had actually increased by 2 ½ times over what it was in 1949 when the People's Republic was founded. In the 30 years from 1949 to 1978 the population doubled. But in the next 30 years it only went up 40%.(38) The 400 million fewer babies born allowed the government to increase its spending on infrastructure such as education and health. Sometime between now and 2050 their total population will actually start to reduce. But in 2015 the government allowed two children in order to help fund the growing number of pensioners. Instead of increasing the retirement age, they opted for more children. This, of course, will increase their population, increase climate change and eventually require still more children as these additional workers eventually retire.

"And you mentioned that there were more male babies born than girls because the boys were assumed to be better able to take care of their parents. As we look at the lessons of history we see that economics is perhaps the basic concern of most people. Relative to having more male babies, in many parts of the world we see girls outnumbering boys in colleges. So if the parents' concern is for economic security in their old age, it is highly possible that their daughters will be more economically able than their sons might have been.

"But let's get into my second major concern. If I can get people to list the most important jobs in a society then look at which ones require a license maybe they will begin to see the importance of parenting. What would you list as among the most important jobs of our society? Driving a car, designing a building, building a house, being a dog, having a child, running a nursery school, operating a mortuary--all require a license except one, and it is the most important."

"There are other important jobs that don't require licenses. Legislators, presidents, governors, CEOs, and look at the trouble they have all gotten us into! In fact it looks like our most important jobs don't require licenses. Why?"

"What kind of a license would you require for our leaders?"

"I would certainly think they should have a knowledge of ethics and economics. They should be experts on the Constitution. They should certainly have some knowledge of politics. I would think that a knowledge of world history and American history should be essential. Some basic knowledge of science—physical, biological and socio-psychological—would be highly useful. So maybe, Wreck, you should advocate leaders licenses while you're advocating parents' licenses.

"One thing at a time, Con. I could push for licenses for teenage parents. Licenses might be able to solve part of the problem of teenage pregnancy. We mentioned that the United States has the highest number of teenage births.

"When you think of the government's costs to aid these poor parents and when you realize that so many will stop their education once parenthood occurs, you can see the staggering economic costs to the government from not having educated people to fill the jobs available and to reduce the chance of having to pay jobless benefits. So it's a double negative. Parents can't get out of poverty because of their children and the children that are born into poverty and are likely to repeat their parents' behavior."

"You are certainly going to have some loud voices in opposition. Perhaps you might suggest that the opponents to your plan pay the total costs for any babies born. There are lots of loud voices and they usually expect somebody else to come up with the money for their ideas. I wonder if the legislators should require financial responsibility for the ideas expressed when people use their rights to free speech. There aren't many who will put the money where their mouth is!"

" Good point Lee, but as you indicate most people just want to 'talk the talk' they expect someone else to pick up the tab. But commander you can certainly emphasize the economic and social costs of raising children. The cost of children will certainly conflict with the desires of adults who want to spend their money on bigger cars or houses or vacations. When you talk 'money' it will certainly perk up some ears. And the desire generated by people's drive for success, for financial or vocational power, or for meaningful jobs in research, teaching or civil service, have already slowed birth rates in the developed countries.

CONFRONTING THE SKEPTICS ON GENOCIDE

"Let's move to another area where I know you'll get skeptics. It stands to reason that people will say that your licensing parents ideas are genocidal what do you have to say to that, Wreck?"

"I would say that it is just the opposite because the objective would be to have more humane people, more happy and socially constructive people in the world. And reducing population is definitely the way to save the human race not to destroy it.

"There's no question about some people saying that licensing parents or even reducing the world population is genocidal. This may be particularly true when it relates to Southern Africans where their higher fertility rates are keeping them impoverished and often starving. But fertility rates are often high in Latin America and in many Mid-Eastern countries. Relative to sub-Saharan Africa, I would guess that there would be charges of genocide by many people of African descent in most countries. In Latin America I will probably be challenged by the Catholic Church and in the Mideast I will be called anti-Islamic, except for Israel where I will be called anti-Semitic.

"Interesting that you bring up genocide because it seems to be a constant of our human history. The world wars were genocidal for Europeans and Americans. It was primarily Christians killing Christians. Africa has had more than its share of genocidal wars and racial cleansing actions. Remember when Zimbabwe's president Robert Mugabe, early in his presidency, used his private army, trained in North Korea, to kill and maim members of the PF-ZAPU. At least 3,000 were killed before they gave up and joined him. Pol Pot was killing his countrymen. Mao was doing the same thing in China. They each killed millions of their Asian countrymen.

"It may just be a localized power struggle in a nation or in a neighborhood. Whether it is Tutsis and Hutus in Rwanda or black and Hispanic gangs practicing genocide against their own ethnic neighbors in Los Angeles—it is certainly genocide. In Rwanda 70% of Tutsis were killed, and a total of over a half million died in their conflicts. In the U.S. about 12,000 gang related deaths occur annually. Too many people are living by the sword instead by the mind.

"Another factor that is also genocidal is the preventable deaths of millions of young children. Fifteen years ago, in 2010, 4.8 million children in Sub-Saharan Africa died before the age of 5 every year – that was 9 deaths every minute. With 20% of the world's births, Sub-Saharan Africa accounted for 45% of childhood deaths. Sub-Saharan Africa is the only region in the world where the number of child deaths is rising. So if we can save these babies for living healthy and constructive lives, can you call it genocide?

"The question is—since white, black, brown and yellow people are being continually killed in wars, gang disagreements, revolutions, capital punishments, and ineffective health care—what do we call genocide? If saving humanity is a worthwhile objective and fewer of every ethnic group should be born, is this geno-killing or geno-preserving?

"It's not about race in an ethnic sense, is about race in the human sense—the human race. Many human actions may be considered genocidal. The American Civil War had Caucasians killing Caucasians. The Chinese civil war under Mao was Chinese killing Chinese. In Rwanda it was blacks killing blacks. Most gang fights are among ethnically similar groups. Did you know that black men are six times more likely to be homicide victims as white men, and they are mainly killed by other blacks.(39)

"The burden of overpopulation is heaviest on those of African descent, particularly those living in Africa. If changes are to be made in reducing poverty, it is obvious that those who are poorest will be negatively affected at first, then they will reap the values of their reduced population and more effective family lives and educations."

"It is one thing for a black leader to suggest reducing black populations, or for a Muslim leader to suggest reducing Muslim populations, it is quite another thing if a non-black or non-Muslim suggests the same thing.

"But there's another kind of killing that you are intimating. Maybe we should call it 'pension-icide' because your ideas are going to kill people's pensions, or at least severely wound them. How are you going to confront the people who want to retire early with high pensions?

CONFRONTING SKEPTICS ON RAISING RETIREMENT AGES

"Look at all the trouble they had in Greece when the government wanted to raise retirement ages. People took to the streets as if they were the Spartans of old, throwing rocks and burning buildings. You could understand that people take it hard when the great giver has to tighten the purse strings and search for more coins to fill the empty purse."

"As for having more babies to provide for the pensions of the older people, we suggested long ago that people should provide for their own pensions through adequate contributions during their working lives and by having longer working lives. But the way modern democracies function, especially as the welfare state expands, people want much more than they have put into their governments. Politicians, in order to get elected, promised more than they could possibly deliver.

"We saw this begin to be addressed 15 years ago when Greece nearly went bankrupt and increased its retirement ages a bit. Greece's upward adjustment of retirement ages was nowhere near enough. While some people in Greece could retire as early as 50, their average age was closer to 62. Other European countries had retirement ages in the mid-60s and were increasing their retirement ages even faster than the Greeks. France planned to raise its retirement age from 60 to 62 eight years later. Germany was raising its from 65 to 67. Even the US raised its retirement age for people born after 1962 to age 67.

"Most of the Western world was swimming in debts. The US owed as much as its gross national product. Greece owed 140% of its GDP and Italy 135% of its GDP. A huge portion of the national debt has been used to finance pensions and healthcare. You can understand the problem with pensions, when people pay 7or 8% of their income for their 45 years of work, then retire for 15 or 20 years after age 60 or 65. They have contributed about 3 ½ years of salary, with their early years of contributions being quite low, but then retiring for a number of years with a salary based on their highest years of earning. Even if they retire at 70% of the highest years' salaries within about seven years they would have exhausted their contributions and interest on those contributions. So the state is required to contribute from its general fund 70% of the top salary of the retirees for 8 to 10 more years. So for the average person the nation has promised to pay seven to ten years of the citizen's full salary out of its general fund. But since the government has many other expenses it must borrow to pay what it has promised to its citizens."

"Wait. You lost me on that! Let me see if I can figure out what to mean. If when I was 20 I started working at a job that paid me $20,000 a year. I began contributing to the state 8% of that. So I contributed $1600 that first-year. Then I retire at age 65 with a salary of $100,000 a year. So for that last year I contributed $8000. Now let's assume that there was a gradual increase in pay over the 40 years. So in my 22nd year my pay would have been $60,000. My retirement contribution would have been $4800 per year. So let's assume that that was my average contribution for the 45 years. So my total contributions over my work life would have been about $216,000. Now I retire at age 65 at 70% of my top pay. So my annual income as a retiree would be $70,000. If I live only three more years I will have taken out all of my contributions. But let's assume that they earned interest at 4%. I would have made another 23 or $24,000 on interest. So that means that I would have contributed enough to pay my pension for a total of about three years and four months. If I live as long as the average retiree the government will have to borrow at least $700,000 to pay for my last 10 years of life.

"So if I were to pay my full retirement from my salary contributions, I would really have to pay about 25% of my monthly salary. Whew! I don't think there are many people who want to pay 25% of their gross income every month. But I guess that's what it would cost if I were to pay my fair share."

"You get the point, Lee. But it is actually worse than that because people keep living longer every decade. For the last 165 years there has been a straight line graph indicating our increasing lifespans. And, if you have followed the Social Security

Administration's life expectancy projections, as I have, you will see that they consistently underestimate the actual life expectancies of Americans. This then makes it look like there is more money in the trust fund than there actually is. So a few years ago the administration said they would not have problems until 2080. But each year that estimate has been reduced as the realities of payouts forced reevaluations. Ten years ago, in 2015, they started to predict more realistically. They predicted that outgo would be greater than income this year, in 2025, and in eight more years the trust fund would be used up. Switzerland has already used up its pension funds. In fact all of us in countries where social welfare has been voted in have troubles—except for Norway.

"Our democratic systems in the West give the voters what they want—early retirements and high pensions. High taxes in Europe make it more possible to handle it—but they still need to raise retirement ages, and they are not doing it fast enough. In our country our selfishness and lack of economic knowledge creates a much greater problem.

"Let's look at medical costs. Of course, Lee, you would want to pay your way medically. In the US the average yearly medical cost is between $5,000 and $7000. If you were in a socialized medicine country the costs would be about half of what it is in US. So if you wanted to pay your way it would take about 10% of your income. So between your retirement and medical expenses are talking about 35% of your pay going into taxes. We won't even mention here the other costs of running the government, like: defense, education, roads, and all the government services. You can see why the Scandinavian countries have tax rates in the high 40%s. Even so they still have national debts at 40 to 60% of their gross domestic products. The US debt to GDP ratio is about 95%, and partially this is because American citizens pay total income taxes in the 10 to 20% range.

"When the realities hit, as it did in Greece in 2010, and will eventually in our country, you can expect that those who were taking more than they were giving will rise in revolt.

AGING POPULATIONS

"One area that the population skeptics often bring up is that the developed world's people are aging. If people are going to be retired it will need young people to pay their retirement benefits. They keep using today's more common retirement ages of 60 to 65 as if they were set in stone. They talk about the world's over 65 population tripling in 25 years, by 2050. By that time one in six people in the world will be over 65. As we talked about earlier, retirement ages must be adjusted upward as our life expectancies increase. It's rather obvious that people are healthier now at age 65 than they were 100 years ago when the average person was dead by that age. And we would certainly expect that a 65-year-old who is expected to live to be 85 would be relatively healthy compared to the 65-year-old of the 1930s. Remember that when the Security Act was passed in America in 1935 the life expectancy was 61.7. So the average person was expected to die three years before collecting his pension. Today people are expected to live 10 to 15 or more years past the time that they retire, if they retire at 67.

"They often point to China where there was a ratio of 16 elderly people per hundred workers in 2010, in 2025 it has doubled to 32, and it will double again by 2050. The problem in our country has been evident for years with Social Security and Medicare having bankrupted their funds. And in 25 years, by 2050, one in six Americans will be over 65. In Europe it will be two of six.

"And you've probably heard of people predicting that our lifespans can be extended almost without limit as we develop artificial hearts, artificial lungs and pancreases, artificial blood cells, artificial joints, et cetera. Heck, we already have a lot of those things.

DO YOU REALLY THINK YOUR PLAN CAN HAPPEN?

"Now Wreck, do you really think either your overpopulation or your parent licensing ideas can be accomplished? And if so, how long would it take?"

"Chet, we don't have any time, and admittedly great things always take time. Shakespeare didn't scribble off Hamlet in an afternoon. Michelangelo took a few years to paint the Sistine Chapel. And how long did it take Homer to formulate his great epics. We need the speed and expertise of an economic Mozart to accomplish the sublime —and the seemingly impossible. The one thing I know is that if I don't do all I can to save our world, my life hasn't been worth living. I remember what Martin Luther King believed. He said that 'The ultimate measure of a man is not where he stands in moments of comfort and convenience, but where he stands at times of challenge and controversy.' He did what he did because of the challenges of his time, and I must pick up the gauntlet and fight for the challenges of my time.

"Realistically I'm pessimistic. Most people think only of their miniscule social and religious nooks and don't want to acknowledge the reality of overpopulation and how it is already affecting them. Politicians in democracies are overwhelmingly concerned with the next election. Businessmen want profits today.

"I must join that small snowball that is already rolling down the hill. We all must become part of that avalanche of realistic fear, cascading down the mountain of inertia--whose rumbles awake the sleeping giants of ignorance and myth. We must be awakened to the reality of the crushing of our earthly home. To escape that avalanche people must move now! You can't wait until your television program is finished, or wait until tomorrow, to escape. People must be awakened from their dreams--that all will be well tomorrow. As comforting as that dream is, thinking minds and the evidence of science clearly show that our planet is in peril— and the fate of our progeny is in our hands, and ours alone.

"The great majority of the people are concerned with their immediate selfish interests. They seem to think that tomorrow will be like yesterday. But today is yesterday's tomorrow and the effects of yesterday's actions are the causes of today's plight and tomorrow's panic. Can we few voices crying in the wilderness wake up the people, their politicians, their priests, and their prophets. I am hopeful. I know that I have to try! It may be an impossible mission, but it must be done. If there ever was a life or death issue, this is it!"

END NOTES

1. Science, Aug 1, 2013 (article by Marshall Burke et al)

1a. United Nations Population Fund report, "State of World Population 2007: Unleashing the Potential of Urban Growth." June 27, 2007

1aa. Arthur Nelson, co-director of the Metropolitan Institute at Virginia Tech, Reported in USA Today, Apr. 30, 2008

1aaa. The State of Food Insecurity in the World 2003, released by UN Food and

Agriculture Organization

2. World Bank projections 2006

2a. Kitzes Current Methods for Calculating National Ecological Footprint Accounts (2007) http://www.brass.cf.ac.uk/uploads/fullpapers/Kitzes

2.   Calhoun, John B. 1962. "Population Density and Social Pathology." Scientific American 206:139-148; and John B. Calhoun. Interview, Los Angeles Times, March 2, 1973

3a. "OECD Employment Outlook 2014: Austerity and the wrong structural reform policies impede growth and employment creation." OECD Employment Outlook 2014. Sept. 3, 2014.

3b. GB Shaw "Everybody's Political What's What?" Ch 9 1944

3.   De Tocqueville. Democracy in America, 1835

4.   Agence France-Presse, February 21, 2006

5.   Mullah Krekar, Aftenposten April 15, 2006

6.   South China Morning Post, November 21, 2005   )

7.   Steven Levitt and Stephen Dubner. *Freakonomics: A Rogue Economist Explores the Hidden Side of Everything.* (2005) William Morrow/Harper Collins

8a. The Times of London, Feb.14, 1009

9.. State ex rel. Swann v. Pack, (42) 527 S.W.2d 99 (Tenn. 1975)

10.   Shenck v. United States, (1919) 249 U.S. 47

11.   Brandenburg v. Ohio [1969] 395 U.S. 444

12.   Cantwell v. State of Connecticut, 310 U.S. 296 (1940).

13.   Goldman v. Weinberger, Secretary of Defense, 475 U.S. 503 (1986)

14.   Gonzales v. O Centro (2006)

546 U.S. 418 15. Buck v. Bell, 274 U.S. 200 (1927)

16.   Skinner v. State of Okl. Ex Rel Williamson, (1942)

316 U.S. 535 16a. Alan Guttmacher Institute.

16b. Haaretz, Oct 18, 2011, New Scientist, Oct 26, 2011

17.   Pierce v School Sisters (1925) 268 US 510

18.   Wisconsin v Yoder (1972) 406 US 205

19.   Deburgh v.Deburgh, (1952(

250 P.2nd 598) 19a. Science Daily. Apr. 20, 2009

20. UN Report 2007

20a. (NASA. Release 10-017, January 21, 2010; See also: http://data.giss.nasa.gov/gistemp/

21. ScienceDaily, Mar. 25, 2005

22. ScienceDaily, Jan. 21, 2009

23. UN REPORT, 2007

24. Wang Qian. China Daily January 28, 2010

25. UN Report, 2007, op.cit

26. Gallop Poll, 2008

27. Jones, J. United Kingdom exporter Guide , 2003, USDA: Nov. 4, 2003.

28. Damien M. Schiff. Earth Day and Overpopulation. Pacific Legal Foundation. Liberty Blog. April 22, 2010

29. Sheldon Richman, Insight on the News, December 20, 1993.

30. Cormac Ó Gráda. Famine: a Short History. Princeton University Press. 2009

31. The FAO Fish and Aquaculture Organisation (2006) http://www.fao.org/fi/default.asp

32. Logic, for those not familiar with the subject, will be discussed in greater

detail
in the Book 8.

33. United Nations World Population Prospects: 2006 revision)

34. Lohan, Tara. AfterNet. Sept. 19, 2009.

35. Murtaugh, PA and Schlax, MG. "Reproduction and the carbon legacies of individuals" Global Environmental Change: 19 (2009) pp. 14-30.

35a. Gullikstad, A. "Villvaeret presser prisene opp" (Wild weather presses the prices up) Dagsavisen Jan. 7, 2011. Pp 18-19

35b. UNITED NATIONS POPULATION FUND (UNFPA). Population and sustainable development�Five years after Rio. New York, UNFPA, 1997. p. 1-36.

36. Kindall, H. and Pimentel, D. Constraints on the Expansion of the Global Food Supply, Ambio--A Journal of Human Environment.. The Royal Swedish Academy of Science: Vol. 23 No. 3, May 1994.

37. USDA's Center for Nutrition Policy and Promotion, 2009.

37a.   http://www.cnpp.usda.gov/calculatorintro.htm

38. Jin Zhu. "China's population set to reach 1.4 billion by 2015. " China Daily. July 5, 2010. Commenting on the report from Li Bin, director of the National Population and Family Planning Commission)

39. FBI statistics 2009

www.ingramcontent.com/pod-product-compliance
Lightning Source LLC
Chambersburg PA
CBHW081327310526
45789CB00018B/2444